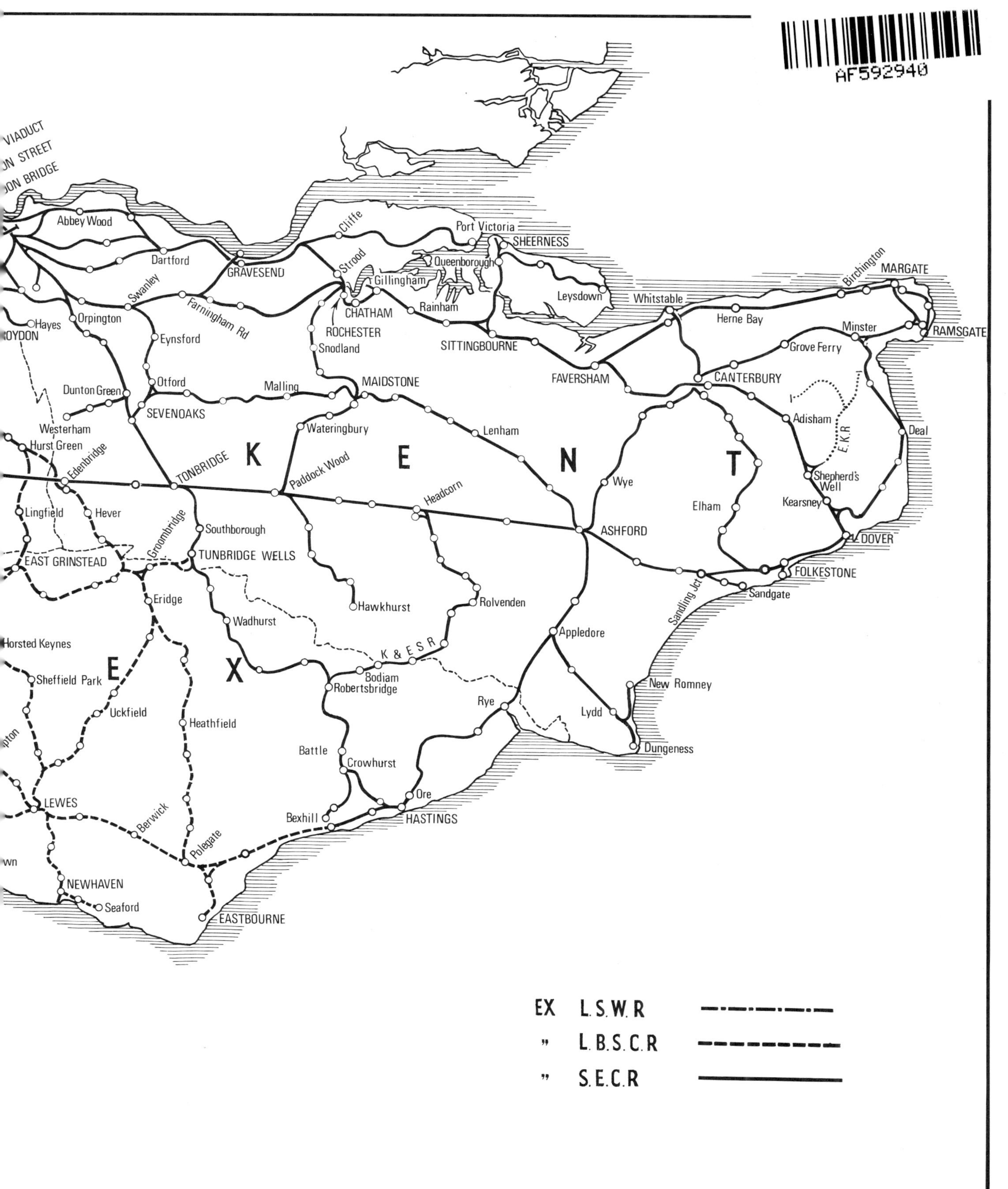

EX	L.S.W.R	–·–·–·–·–
"	L.B.S.C.R	- - - - - - -
"	S.E.C.R	————

Roaming the Southern Rails

DAY
CONTINENTAL
34039

Roaming the Southern Rails

P. Ransome-Wallis

LONDON

IAN ALLAN LTD

First published 1979

ISBN 0 7110 0893 0

Published by Ian Allan Ltd, Shepperton, Surrey; and printed in the United Kingdom by Ian Allan Printing Ltd

Frontispiece: 'West Country' class No 34039 *Boscastle* on loan to the Eastern Region in 1949, heading the Liverpool Street-Harwich 'Day Continental' boat train near Bethnal Green.

Below: Mid-Hants Railway: Class N 2-6-0 No 31874 *Aznar Line* with a train from Ropley to Alresford.

Contents

BY THE SAME AUTHOR

On Railways at Home and Abroad (2 editions)
Locomotives Through the Lens
Men of the Footplate
British Railways To-day
On Engines in Britain and France
Southern Album (2 editions)
Concise encyclopaedia of World Railway Locomotives (Editor and Contributor)
The Last Steam Locomotives of British Railways (4 editions)
The Last Steam Locomotives of Western Europe (2 editions)
The Last Steam Locomotives of Eastern Europe
Preserved Locomotives of Western Europe (Volumes I and II)
The World's Smallest Public Railway — RH&DR (5 editions)
The Snowdon Mountain Railway (3 editions)
All About Photographing Trains (2 editions)
Famous Railway Photographers — P. Ransome-Wallis
Locomotives & Trains of the Big Four
Train Ferries of Western Europe
Ships and the Sea
The Royal Navy (3 editions)
North Atlantic Panorama

Foreword

Shortly before his untimely death in May 1978, the celebrated railway photographer the Rt. Rev. Eric Treacy, contributed the following Foreword to this book

For as long as I have been interested in railway photography the name Ransome-Wallis has been amongst the 'greats'. His interest in railways goes back to his early childhood and his schooldays in York provided ample opportunity for this interest to flourish.

Ransome-Wallis has covered many thousands of miles in order to study and to photograph locomotives the world over and railway enthusiasts are immensely in his debt for the excellent pictures he has produced.

Living, as he does, in Herne Bay the Southern Region is very much his home pitch and, having seen the prints he has selected, I am confident that those who come into possession of this book will share my pleasure in studying his presentation of motive power on the Southern. I am particularly glad that his remit included Southern ports and harbours, for this has brought a refreshing variety to his selection of pictures.

Finally, may I express my pleasure that Ransome-Wallis agreed to contribute to this series of 'Roaming' books. I am confident that this book will receive a great welcome from all those to whom his name and his work have been well known for more than half a century.

ERIC TREACY
(Editorial Adviser of the 'Roaming' series)

Right: Boat train for SS *Queen Elizabeth 2* arriving at the Southampton Ocean Terminal. Class 74 Bo-Bo electro-diesel No 74.001 rebuilt from a dc electric locomotive of Class 71.

Queen Elizabeth 2
74 001

Introduction

When Eric Treacy asked me to compile the Southern book in his 'Roaming' series, I hesitated for a long time before accepting because Treacy's approach to locomotive and train photography is quite different from mine. His work has great artistic merit (his photographs have been exhibited in the London Salon) while mine is concerned primarily with technical aspects of locomotives and the duties on which they are employed. His is pictorial art, mine is documentary record.

I accepted the assignment because perhaps, what my photographs lack in artistic merit, they may gain in railway interest and adequately portray motive power at work and at rest. I was often unlucky with 'smoke effects' and, unless I had previously 'bribed' the fireman, the photogenic clouds usually appeared before or after passing me! Even those notorious smoke-producers the Bulleid Pacifics, have more often than not gone by me with beautifully clear chimney tops!

My railway photography began in the summer of 1917 and my first photograph was of a Sheffield to Lincoln train on the Great Central line near Shireoaks. The camera was a box Brownie, the film Kodak Non-Curling and I still have that negative. I have long since taken many worse pictures with far more elaborate and expensive cameras. I have owned and worked with many cameras but never with a film size less than 6 x 9cm, except in colour in which I use 6 x 6cm. For years I carried with me a ¼-plate reflex usually with 36 loaded dark slides. A lot of weight but in my younger days I thought nothing of it and even carried it on my back during a six-week motorcycle tour of seven European countries in 1929. I was adept at changing the plates in my dark slides beneath the bedclothes! Later I owned a VN 9 x 12cm Press camera but my favourite for speed work was a 6 x 9cm Deckrullo with the finest lens of all, a Zeiss Tessar f3.5 which, of course, was not 'bloomed'.

For pictures in which very fast shutter speeds are not required I have always had at least one 6 x 9cm bellows-type roll film camera and I now have four in regular use. Three of these are used with black and white film and they are: a Super Ikonta with Tessar f3.5; a Bessa II with Color-Skopar f3.5 and another Bessa II with an Apo-Lanthar f4.5 lens — this is the best of the three. All have Compur Rapid shutters which are maintained to give accurate speeds. Colour is of secondary importance to me but I get very acceptable results from a Selfix-820 with a good Ross Xpres f3.8 lens. This is an excellent British camera, bought new for £24 in 1948. I use the built-in masks to give 6 x 6cm transparencies on Agfa CT I8 film.

My monochrome roll films are Ilford and I use both HP4 and FP4 usually carrying two cameras with a different film in each one. I have tried most makes of roll film and I find the Ilford emulsion most suitable for my work, despite some batches having far too many manufacturing faults. I always dish develop my films and inspect them in a green safelight before fixing. I have only once tried to use a tank for roll film and gave up when the film somehow got tangled round my legs! However, I always use a Dallan tank for developing cut-film or plates. My developer is usually Kodak D-76 used half-strength at 68°F or, if I am in a hurry, Unitol is quite satisfactory.

Bearing in mind that my work is mainly 'record' the locomotive or the train is the subject which must be clearly presented and clouds and engine exhaust are of minor importance to me. I dislike telegraph poles and other excrescences appearing above the locomotive and these are invariably blocked out with Photopake. The resulting white image on the print is eradicated by careful use of iodo-cyanide reducer applied with a brush while the print is damp. This gives a dead-white sky but can, in suitable cases, be so applied as to produce very convincing clouds. Needless to say I meticulously spot-out all pinholes on the negative and I retouch these on the print with special water-colour.

For reproduction, I provide prints with plenty of contrast but without loss of shadow detail and if this is threatened, I reduce the darkest areas, again with iodo-cyanide. I also like to emphasise some relevant parts of a print by retouching or lining-in with water colour. Colour transparencies with offensively bright highlights I find can be successfully subdued with dilute Martin's grey dye.

I have a Wasp III enlarger which can cope with all negative sizes from 5½ x 3½ to 2¾ x 2¾in and I have a lens of different focal length for use with extension tubes for reduction or for enlargement from 35mm negatives. I have also made very good black and white negatives from some of my colour transparencies.

My collection amounts to about 15,000 negatives of railways taken all over the world and some 5,000 negatives of ships. Prints are made to postcard size and most are mounted in loose-leaf slip-in albums made specially for me. Some are mounted in special interleaved card mounts. The title of each print with its negative number is micro-typed on white paper, cut to size and inserted firmly into the relative mount. All negatives are enveloped and carry corresponding numbers. They are filed in special wood drawers.

I quite enjoy my photography but always it has been a means to an end — photography with a purpose and my over-riding interest has always been the *subject*, be it railway locomotive or ship.

Below: BR Standard Class 4 2-6-0 heads a Salisbury to Portsmouth train near Fareham in 1957.

About this book

British Railways has been, like so many nationalised industries in Britain, a political shuttlecock and it has been reorganised by various brands of politicians, I think eight times in 30 years. (No wonder it's in debt!) The reorganisations have usually included alterations to the regional boundaries and sometimes the creation of new regions or the deletion of old ones. So which area should one describe when *Roaming The Southern Rails?* Greatly daring, I have opted for the present boundaries though probably by the time this book is in print another gaggle of politicians may have decided that York should be included in the Southern! Who knows?

The present Southern differs from former Southerns by stopping at Salisbury in the West but going on to Weymouth in the South. In spite of my intention to adhere to present boundaries I could not resist the temptation to include a few pictures taken west of Salisbury, an area which has always held much charm and the best of the Southern scenery.

I have lived the last 45 years of my life at Herne Bay on the North Kent coast. Understandably, therefore, the largest section of the book deals with the Eastern Division of the Southern, that is mainly the territory of the former South Eastern & Chatham Railway. The route mileage of this railway was 625 against the 862 miles of the London & South Western (the South Western Division) and 431 miles of the London Brighton & South Coast (the Central Division). The Eastern Division, however, carries a great deal of main line traffic and had a large variety of steam motive power.

Things have greatly changed today for the Southern Region generally has less variety in its motive power than any of the other regions. Its main line diesel fleet is composed of only Class 33 (with sub-divisions); there is a class of electro-diesels but its electric locomotives have all been withdrawn. (A number of Class 47 diesel-electric locomotives regularly work in from other regions). For the rest, trains are composed of third rail electric and diesel-electric multiple-units which, while being very efficient, are not in any way photogenic!

In three books published in the last ten years I have described and illustrated Southern locomotives of the pre-nationalisation era. In this book the emphasis is on the more recent forms of motive power — steam, diesel and electric. In doing this I have revisited locations where, 20 and more years ago, I have taken many successful pictures. How different are these places today! Not only is it impossible to reach the lineside — stout fencing protects Southern 'roamers' from the dangers of the electric third rail — but trees, shrubs and undergrowth in profusion have blanketted the view of the track. In the old days such obstructions were kept in check by sparks from steam locomotives which caused lineside fires. Now, in many areas, it is necessary to hire private contractors to cut back the growth.

I have not attempted to describe or to illustrate the vast network of Southern suburban lines — these warrant a volume of their own, (*Roaming Southern Suburbia?*). I have illustrated some of the privately owned railways in the Region and also some of the Preservation lines, three of which are in Kent.

The Southern has always been closely associated with the sea and shipping and, indeed, owned a considerable fleet of cross-channel ships. Furthermore, the development of the great dock system at Southampton was almost entirely a Southern Railway concept and was largely due to the initiative and foresight of one of the world's most able railwaymen, the late Sir Herbert Walker. While in a book of this sort it is impossible to do justice to this aspect of Southern activities I have included a number of photographs of ships and harbours relevant to my Southern Roaming.

Finally, it is necessary to admit that some of the photographs in this book have been published before. How many, I cannot say, as I do not keep a record of those of my photographs which appear in magazines and in books other than my own. Certainly only three or four which have appeared in my books over the last 10 years are now repeated and those few are either unique, unusual or highly relevant.

South Eastern Territory in Kent

The intricate network of railways in Kent inherited by the Southern in 1923 was almost entirely that of the South Eastern & Chatham Railway. The incredible complications and duplications of the routes of this railway were brought about by the uninhibited and ruinous competition between the South Eastern and the London Chatham and Dover Railways which, when both were nearly bankrupt in 1899, together formed the SE&C which was run by a Managing Committee composed of directors from each of the constituent companies.

For present purposes, it is convenient to describe our Kentish roaming in four parts, the first two of which are based on the territory served, respectively, by each of the old companies while the third deals with the important and lucrative traffic to the Channel ports in which both companies had a share. The fourth part concerns the privately owned railways in Kent.

The South Eastern owned the two important London termini, Charing Cross and Cannon Street, both of which are on the north bank of the River Thames. The tracks from each station come together at Borough Market Junction a short distance to the north of London Bridge station, the 'through' part of which also belonged to the South Eastern. When railway friends from abroad come to visit me, I take them during the rush-hour, either to London Bridge or to Clapham Junction at either of which they will see a concentration of traffic, suburban and main line, unequalled anywhere else in Europe.

From London Bridge the main line heads south east and, at the suburban station of St John's begins the long and almost unbroken climb, much of it at 1 in 120, to Knockholt nearly 11 miles further on. Near Chislehurst, about six miles from St John's, the line passes over the former LC&D main line from Victoria to the Kent Coast and points east. Here junctions provide access to loop lines which connect the two main lines in each direction. It is in this area that some of our most expert railway photographers have made many of their best pictures.

After passing Knockholt the line enters Polhill Tunnel at the beginning of a falling gradient which persists, except for a short rise before Sevenoaks, nearly all of the 12 miles to Tonbridge. Tonbridge station is approached by a severe curve and up trains, having reduced speed are then faced with a climb of five miles at 1 in 122 to Sevenoaks Tunnel in which, although the gradient eases a little, the rails are often greasy and wet. I have travelled on many locomotives which have slipped so badly in the two-mile-long tunnel that it has been 'touch and go' whether we should stall completely. The 'West Country' class were the most vulnerable and I have a very vivid recording which I made in 1960 on the footplate of No 34005 *Barnstaple* with the up 'Golden Arrow'. Only the most expert handling by the driver prevented an undignified unscheduled stop.

Tonbridge is an important junction. Coming in from the west is the SE line from Reading via Redhill and which, for nearly 20 miles between Redhill and Tonbridge, is almost dead straight. Then, soon after passing through the station, the line to Hastings via Tunbridge Wells and Robertsbridge goes off in a southerly direction. The loading gauge on this line is restricted due to reduced clearances through tunnels on the line although that at Mountfield has been overcome by singling the track. This Hastings line is also difficult from a locomotive viewpoint; the ruling gradient is 1 in 47 going south and 1 in 45 for a short distance in the up direction. The 'Schools' class gave many distinguished performances on this line.

East of Tonbridge for 26 miles the going is easy in both directions and high speeds are possible. Paddock Wood, 5½ miles east was the junction for the Hawkhurst line, now closed and then, running north, is the interesting line through Maidstone, Strood and on to become the North Kent line to

Gravesend, Dartford and Hither Green to reach the London termini. In the two-mile long Strood Tunnel the track is laid on the filled-in bed of a canal.

Ashford is where the South Eastern built its locomotives. The works there completed its first locomotive in 1853 and went on to build and repair locomotives for the SE&C and then the Southern. After nationalisation, locomotive work continued until electrification in 1961 since when the works has been used for the construction and repair of freight vehicles for service at home and overseas. The extensive running sheds on the other side of the line have been demolished — one has many happy memories of visits there to photograph engines fresh out of works.

Joining the SE lines to the west of Ashford station is the LC&D line from Swanley Junction via Maidstone East. An important line this as it affords a rational and much used alternative route for continental traffic to and from Victoria. Then, just east of the station, another line to Hastings goes off to the south. This line is routed via Appledore (where another branch leaves for Dungeness and formerly New Romney) and Rye. A little further east from Ashford, the line to Ramsgate and Margate via Canterbury West turns northwards from the main line. Until 1947, a line from Cheriton via Elham joined the line south of Canterbury West. Also from this station the famous Canterbury and Whitstable line originally was opened in 1830. It was closed to traffic in 1952 but was reopened for a few months in 1953 when the Kent Coast line was severely damaged by floods.

Twenty miles to Dover Marine and again there is some climbing to do until, after passing Westenhanger the route is downhill for the final 12 miles. In the old days, this long incline, though not severe, (ruling at 1 in 250) could be quite awkward for some engines starting 'cold' from Dover with a heavy up train.

After passing Folkestone Junction, at which point the branch down to Folkestone Harbour leaves the main line, the last few miles are almost on the seashore, running along the foot of the 'white cliffs' and through three tunnels where those cliffs protrude southwards towards the sea. Shortly before reaching the Marine station, a short loop curves northwards to join the old LC&D line from Dover Priory. (Trains from Ramsgate to Charing Cross via Deal and Folkestone use this loop), after which a right-hand curve leads into Dover Marine station.

Below: Cannon Street station in 1959 with, left to right, No 30920 *Rugby* on a Ramsgate train, No 1035 a Hastings 6-car diesel-electric unit and No 30923 *Bradfield* leaving for Dover.

Top right: Ashford station was always a very interesting place in the days of steam and indeed it still is. In this 1952 photograph a 3-cylinder 2-6-0 of Class U1 No 31904 is coming off the up main line on to the up platform road with a semi-fast from Dover. On the left is Class E1 No 31506 awaiting a train for Canterbury West and Ramsgate while a Class H 0-4-4T is seen shunting on the right of the view.

Bottom right: Margate to Charing Cross train composed of two 4-CEP units entering the up main line platform at Ashford, Kent. On the up main line is Class 08 0-6-0 diesel-electric shunter No 08.414.

332
89
31506
7211
4
UE 96

D6526
4

Above left: Charing Cross to Margate fast train passing Ashford marshalling yard. Type 3 Bo-Bo diesel-electric No D6526 (later 33.017).

Left: Chart Leacon Maintenance Depot at Ashford is concerned mainly with main line electric multiple units.

Above: 'Schools' class No 30932 *Blundells* was fitted with a high-sided tender when, in 1951, it was photographed working an up Folkestone express passing Paddock Wood.

Centre right: Class U No 31627 at Ashford in 1949 with no insignia on the tender. This locomotive was one of the series built new as tender engines and was not a rebuild of a 'River' class tank locomotive.

Bottom right: Class N 2-6-0 No 31848 was working a heavy coal train when photographed on the up main line near Marden in 1954.

Top left: Sandling Junction on the Dover-London main line, used to be the origin of a branch line to Hythe and Sandgate. This was closed in December 1951 and the main line station dropped 'Junction' from its name. An up train from Dover in charge of No 30935 *Sevenoaks* is seen here leaving.

Centre left: An unusual double-heading was seen on an up slow train passing Westenhanger in 1961 when an 01 class 0-6-0, No 31065 was pilot to 'Schools' class No 30934 *St Lawrence.* The old engine was to work an LCGB excursion from Tonbridge the next day.

Below: Charing Cross to Margate train composed of one 4-CEP unit leaving Shakespeare Cliff Tunnel.

Right: A train from Ramsgate to Ashford near Sturry was in charge of an ex-LMS 2-6-4T No 42096 when it met an ex-Southern Railway Class N 2-6-0 working an eastbound freight in 1956.

Below right: Train of coal empties for Betteshanger Colliery passing Sandwich. Class 73/0 electro-diesel No 73.127.

5K

Above: Margate to Dover and Charing Cross train leaving Deal in 1954. 'Schools' class No 30936 *Cranleigh* with single blastpipe.

Right: 'Schools' class 3-cylinder 4-4-0 No 30920 *Rugby* heading a Ramsgate-Dover Priory-Ashford-Charing Cross train on the 1 in 60 descent to Buckland Junction in 1948.

Below right: SAGA special train empties from Margate to Ashford passing Minster Junction behind Class 33/0 Bo-Bo diesel-electric No 33.055.

Left: Brighton to Ore electric train composed of two 4-CIG units, leaving Hastings Tunnel.

Below: Hastings to Charing Cross Class 203 6-car diesel-electric unit No 1036 approaching Battle.

Above: Redhill to Reading train composed of SE&C 'birdcage' stock, leaving Dorking Town in 1949. Class N 2-6-0 No 31863 was still in Southern colours.

Right: Hastings to Ashford freight train passing the old windmill at Rye in 1948. Class C 0-6-0 No 31038.

Below right: Hawkhurst branch pick-up freight near Paddock Wood in 1959. Class C No 31721 was in charge.

Above: The little Wainwright Class H 0-4-4Ts were among the most useful engines of the SE&CR. Seen here is No 31327 working a Paddock Wood to Maidstone train leaving Yalding in 1951.

Left: Canterbury & Whitstable *Invicta* of 1830 preserved at Canterbury. This locomotive has now been moved to the York Railway Museum.

Right: Working a train for Ramsgate in 1950, No 796 *Sir Dodinas Le Savage* (with 6-wheeled tender) was passing under the ex-SER Canterbury and Whitstable line, east of Whitstable while a rebuilt Stirling 0-6-0T Class R1 BR No 31069 headed a freight from Whitstable Harbour to Canterbury West.

Below: Class R1 No 31339 taking water from a stand-pipe at Whitstable Harbour in 1950.

The London Chatham & Dover Main Line

The LC&D was the smaller and poorer constituent of the SE&C. It came on the scene later than did the South Eastern and its history was complicated and difficult. It had two London termini, Victoria which served the West End and Holborn Viaduct the City. Tracks from these stations converge and join at Herne Hill. The 79¼ miles of the main line from Victoria to Ramsgate have many gradients and the long speed restrictions through the Medway towns prevent any very fast start-to-stop timings. During the steam era many trains were tightly timed and it required a high standard of driving skill to maintain those schedules. The fastest train was the 'Granville Express' which took 90 minutes non-stop for the 73¾ miles to Margate. The best timing for the same distance by electric traction is 95 minutes but with no fewer than eight intermediate stops.

For down trains the difficulties for steam trains began at Victoria where immediately there is the steep and curving incline at 1 in 62 up to Grosvenor Bridge. The 'cold start' was usually aided by a banking engine which had brought the empty stock into the platform. Having crossed the bridge, the gradients are mostly against the engine for the next 5½ miles culminating in 1¾ miles at 1 in 100 before Penge Tunnel after which the line falls at 1 in 330.

Most trains stop at Bromley South and for down trains this means starting away on a mile-long gradient of 1 in 95. The 'King Arthurs' usually got away without slipping as did the Standard Class 5s. The 'Schools' sometimes slipped badly if the driver was 'ham-fisted', but the un-rebuilt 'West Countries' hardly ever made a clean start. The electrics have automatic slip control and the gradient presents no problems. Soon after the top is reached the LC&D line passes under the SE main line and there are connecting loops between the two lines in both directions.

Swanley Junction is 17½ miles from Victoria and here the line to Maidstone East and Ashford goes off southwards. After passing Swanley, down trains have their first opportunity for really fast running and the next three miles at 1 in 100 down to Farningham Road could be quite exciting on the footplate with speeds often in the eighties and then with enough momentum to get up the ensuing 1 in 100 without any problems. Nearly 10 miles from Swanley Junction, Sole Street is reached and the summit of what is, for up trains, the most difficult section of the route from the coast. Difficult, but also the most beautiful part of the journey with the Medway Valley stretching out below the railway and a fine view of the city of Rochester with its bridges, its cathedral and its castle.

From Sole Street to Rochester Bridge Junction the gradient is at 1 in 100 down for six miles at the end of which there is a severe curve where speed is restricted to 30mph before the South Eastern North Kent-Maidstone line is crossed by a bridge. Then over the Medway Bridge, past Rochester station and a fine view of the port and its shipping before entering Fort Pitt Tunnel which, in steam days, was rather foul and suffered from the noisy roar of rail corrugations. So into the murky greyness of Chatham station.

For London-bound steam trains starting away from Chatham, the next 7½ miles required a good engine and a good crew if time was to be kept, especially with a full load and a wet rail. With the 30mph restriction before the six-mile climb to Sole Street it was impossible to get a 'run at the bank' and even electrics have been known to fail before reaching the summit. In my experience the Standard Class 5 4-6-0s consistently gave the best performances; 'West Country's' were prone to slipping as also were the 'Schools' unless carefully handled. My own 'footplate record' was in June 1937 when I travelled on 'Lord Nelson' No 855 *Robert Blake* with a train of eight coaches + two bogie vans (about 300 tons full). We started the climb at 42mph and, with a full regulator and about 35 per cent cut-

off, *accelerated* to 59mph at the summit with the engine blowing-off!

Proceeding eastwards after leaving Chatham are three more tunnels before reaching Gillingham where there used to be an engine shed with, usually, some elderly tender engines on view. Sittingbourne, 9½ miles further on, is the junction for the line to Sheerness which now crosses the Swale by a lifting bridge which replaced the Scherzer rolling-lift bridge in 1959.

At Faversham the line divides, one line going southeast to Canterbury East, Dover Priory and Dover Marine, while the other reaches the Kent Coast two miles west of Whitstable. In the down direction, the start from Whitstable is up at 1 in 87 for ½ mile while, from Herne Bay, the gradient is 1 in 93 against the engine for the 1½ miles of Blacksole Bank. Before World War II, weekend traffic to the coast was very heavy and from Blacksole Bridge it was often possible to have four down trains in sight at the same time with, like as not, a different class of locomotive on each train. Small wonder that many summer Saturdays were spent on the lineside near Blacksole Summit — with such a parade of motive power there was certainly no point in roaming to other locations!

Across the Reculver Marshes, the line is laid along the sea-wall which was built in 1953 after the track had been washed away for nearly two miles during the disastrous floods of that February.

Margate station was originally the LC&D 'Margate West'. It was reconstructed and modernised during the early years of the Southern Railway being opened in its present form in July 1926. At the same time the old South Eastern terminal station, Margate Sands, was closed. Starting away from Margate the gradient is against the engine, ruling at 1 in 110 to Broadstairs.

The LC&D station at Ramsgate was known as the Harbour station. It was nearly on the beach and was reached by a falling gradient of 1 in 75 most of which was in tunnel. The SE station was also a terminus known as Ramsgate Town. Trains from Ashford and from Dover via Deal arrived at this station where they reversed to complete the journey to Margate Sands. The Southern Railway closed both these stations and lifted the SE track to Margate Sands. A connecting line was built to join up the lines of the former rivals, and at the western end of this line, the present through station at Ramsgate is situated.

The results of the intense rivalry between the SE and LC&D were of inestimable value to the country in both world wars. There were alternative routes to almost all Southern stations and especially to the vitally important Channel ports. So the bombing and the shelling never had quite such a serious effect on the railways in Kent which in other circumstances could have been disastrous.

Left: The approaches to Victoria station, London. Top centre: Grosvenor Bridge, top left Battersea power station and below this can be seen the carriage sheds. In the foreground the steam locomotive yard.

Below: Nearing the end of the 5-mile climb at 1 in 100, No 30769 *Sir Balan* was going well when approaching Sole Street with an up Ramsgate train in 1959.

Top left: Although the Class N1 3-cylinder 2-6-0s were essentially freight engines, they not infrequently appeared on passenger trains. No 31880 was starting the 5-mile climb to Sole Street with an up return excursion from Margate in 1959.

Centre left: This Gillingham to Victoria train about to ascend Sole Street bank was composed of three 2-HAP units.

Below: Standard Class 5 No 73085 was photographed at Rochester working a down fast train to the Kent Coast only two weeks before the service was electrified in 1959. On the right is 2-6-2T No 41313 at the head of a slow train from Strood to Faversham.

Right: Rebuilt 'West Country' No 34003 *Plymouth* entering Chatham with a Cannon Street-Ramsgate express in 1959.

Below right: One of the first of the 'Schools' class, No 30901 *Winchester* with a multiple-jet blastpipe, was working an up Kent Coast train when photographed in 1959 entering Chatham.

30912

30938
374

7139
7139
50
HE MAN OF KENT

Above, far left: The driver of No 30912 *Downside* awaits the 'Right Away' from Chatham. Ahead is Fort Pitt Tunnel.

Above left: Leaving Sittingbourne in 1959 with an up Ramsgate train was Class V No 30938 *St Olave's* with Bulleid-Lemaître exhaust.

Left: Victoria to Ramsgate train composed of three 4-CEP units leaving Sittingbourne. Right is 'Deltic' Class 55 No 55.007 *Pinza* which was heading a special train on 26 March 1978.

Above: Small boys still find interest in the railway even though electric multiple units have none of the glamour of steam. Here, their interest is in a down Kent Coast fast train composed of two 4-CEP and one 4-BEP units passing Stone Crossing.

Right: No 30772 *Sir Percivale* began blowing off when the driver shut off steam on sighting a distant at 'on' near Teynham in 1953. The train, composed of LNER stock was an excursion from York to Margate.

Above left: In filthy condition and having steaming problems, No 30793 *Sir Ontzlake* was struggling with a down Margate excursion in 1956 near Teynham.

Left: The business trains between Ramsgate and Cannon Street usually had the best rolling stock and ran to very tight schedules. Rebuilt 'West Country' Pacific No 34005 *Barnstaple* was passing through the Kentish orchards near Teynham with a Cannon Street to Ramsgate express in 1958.

Above: Class C, No 31268 was working an up semi-fast train from Dover and was photographed near Stone Crossing in 1952.

Right: Excursion train from Hull to Margate passing Faversham Junction. Brush/Sulzer Class 47/0 Co-Co diesel-electric No 47.180. The catenary seen in the right background was for Southern electric locomotives which could use their pantographs when shunting in freight yards with no third rail. The electro-diesels made this system redundant.

Above: Up Ramsgate train photographed near Chestfield in 1957. 'Schools' class No 30936 *Cranleigh.*

Right: Standard Class 5 No 73086 is here seen at the head of a 10-coach up Kent Coast express near Chestfield in 1956. The picture shows two electrically-operated intermediate block signals — one for the down road on the left and one for the up, seen above the last coach of the train.

Below right: On the first day of the Kent Coast electrification (15 June 1959) personnel from the operating, signalling and mechanical and electrical engineer's departments made several trips in the area. They travelled in the ex-L&SW's director's saloon hauled by Type 2 Bo-Bo diesel-electric No D5011 (later Class 24/0 No 24.011), seen here near Chestfield.

Far right, top: The 8-car down 'Kentish Belle' was in charge of Class V No 30929 *Malvern* with Bulleid-Lemaître exhaust when photographed near Chestfield in 1958.

Far right, bottom: At the head-end of a down Kent Coast train in 1956, No 30795 *Sir Dinadan* was 'panned' by the camera near Whitstable.

1&2
30929
PULLMAN
30795

Above: Down excursion train for Margate running alongside the seashore near Seasalter. Birmingham/Sulzer Class 33/0 Bo-Bo diesel-electric No 33.048.

Centre left: With no exhaust visible when leaving Herne Bay on a hot summer's day in 1938, 'Lord Nelson' class No 863 *Lord Rodney* was heading an up slow train from Ramsgate to Victoria.

Bottom left: After being exhibited at the Festival of Britain from 4 May until 30 September 1951, No 70004 *William Shakespeare* worked some 'running-in' turns between Victoria and Ramsgate before taking up regular duties on the 'Golden Arrow'. Here it is approaching Herne Bay with an up slow train of four coaches.

Above right: A historic picture at Herne Bay! The first working of a 'Merchant Navy' class Pacific on the Kent Coast line was made by No 21C7 *Aberdeen Commonwealth* in October 1944 and I was lucky enough to choose the train to travel home on leave after a spell in the North Atlantic.

Right: The centenary of the opening of the LC&D line from Herne Bay to Ramsgate was celebrated by the carrying of a headboard attached to the 07.40 train from Victoria on 7 October 1963. British Railways provided excellent hospitality to civic dignitaries and a good time was had by all!

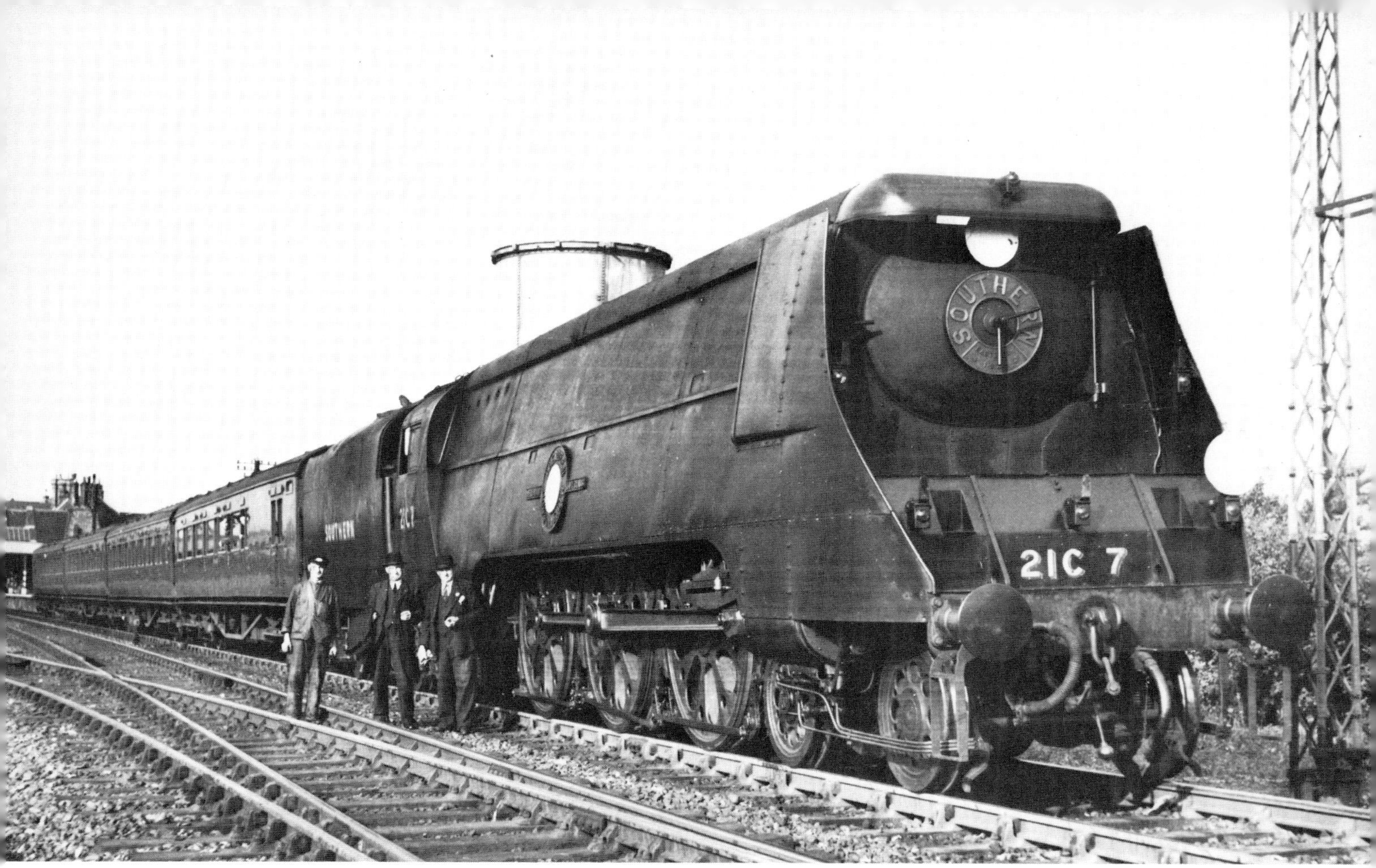

SOUTHERN
21C 7
SOUTHERN
21C 7

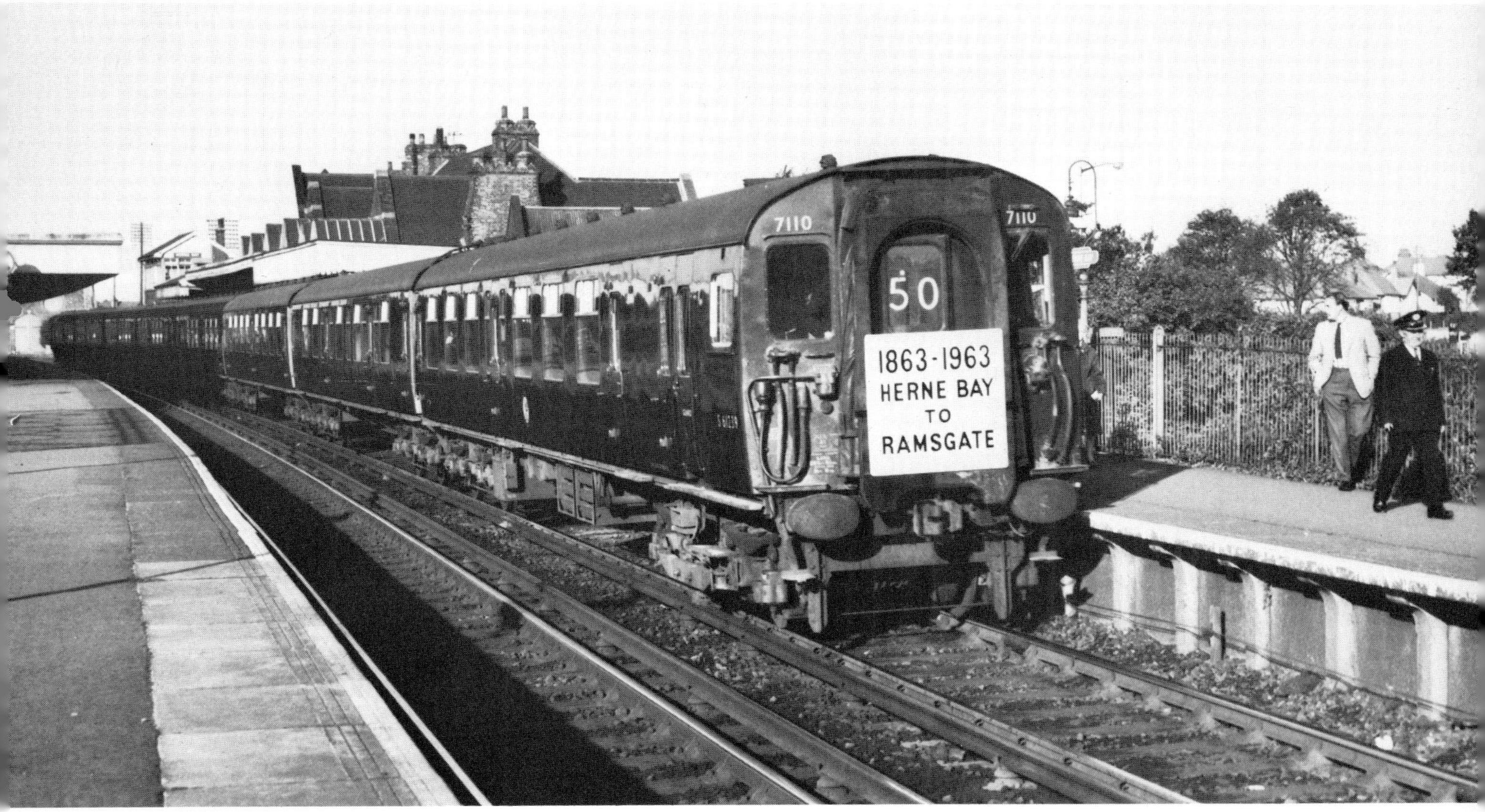

7110
7110
50
1863-1963
HERNE BAY
TO
RAMSGATE

Top right: No 31715, ex-SE&C Class C was shunting the mid-day local freight at Herne Bay in 1959, shortly before the 'electrics' took over.

Centre right: In 1936 the non-superheater Class E 4-4-0s were regular performers on the Southern's North Kent routes and No 1166 was heading for Margate with a Sunday excursion.

Below: Class BB No 21C157 *Biggin Hill* was making light work of hauling the 10-car 'Thanet Belle' up Blacksole Bank in 1948.

Above: With a locomotive inspector on the footplate and a special saloon behind the tender, Class E1 No 1179 was working a down Kent Coast Pullman Car train up Blacksole Bank in 1935.

Left: Cardiff to Margate excursion train at Blacksole Summit. Brush/Sulzer Class 47/0 Co-Co diesel-electric No 47.077 *North Star.*

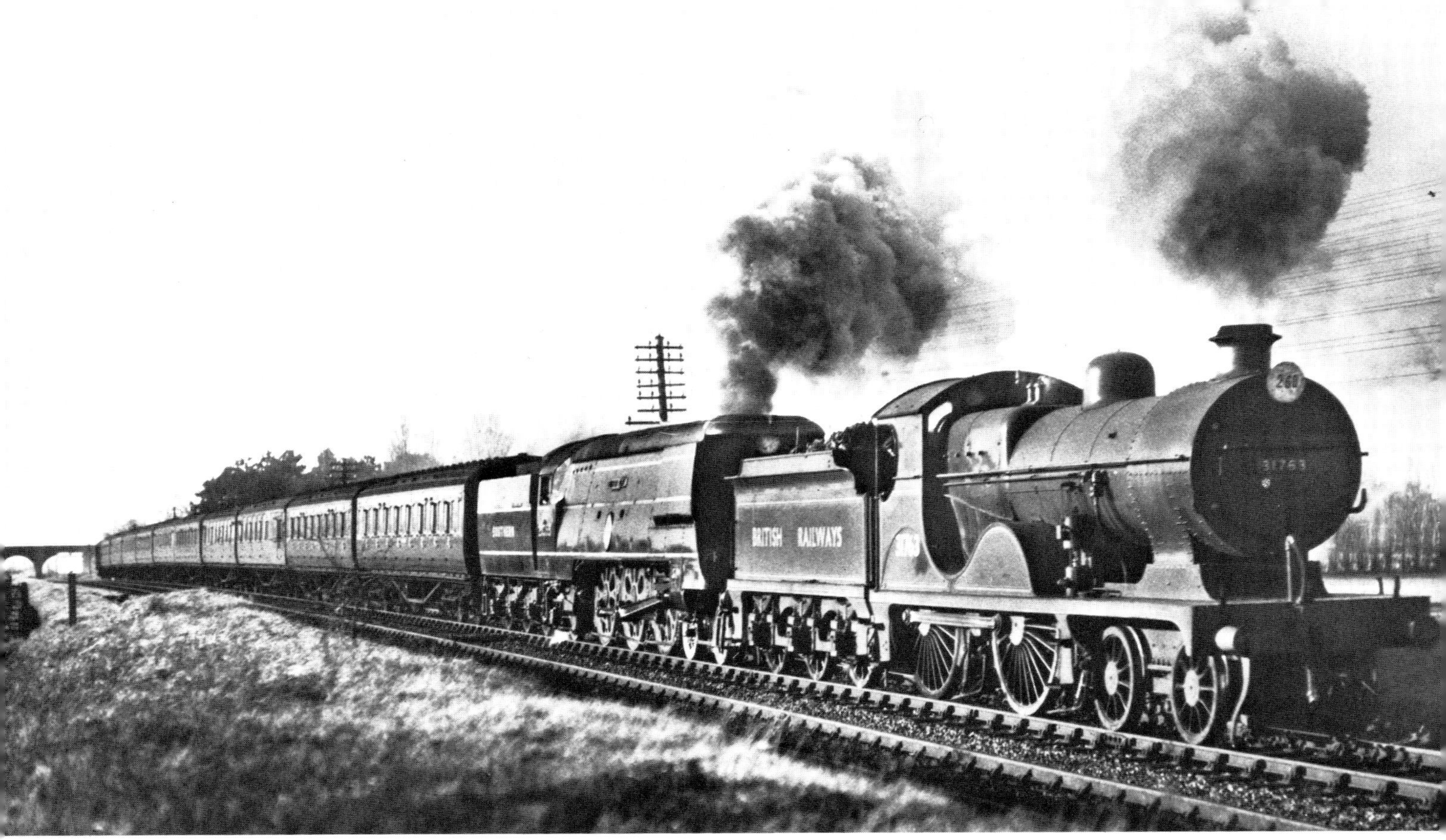
BRITISH RAILWAYS
31763

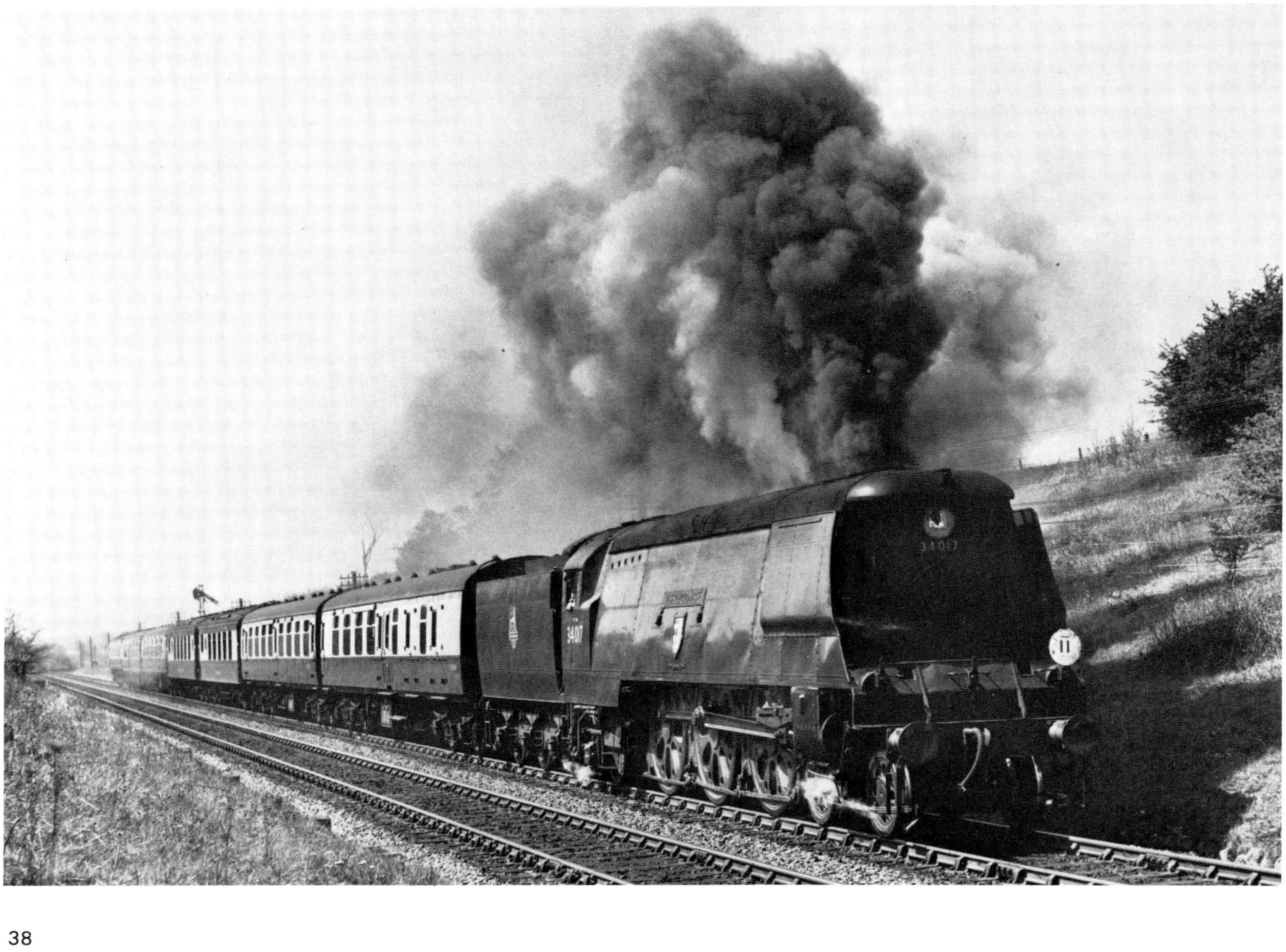
34017

Above left: Christmas Day 1948! A Class L 4-4-0 No 31763 was pilot to 'Battle of Britain' No 21C155 *Fighter Pilot* on a Victoria to Ramsgate train near Herne Bay.

Left: Environmental pollution was obviously not considered when No 34017 *Ilfracombe* was climbing Blacksole Bank with 5 coaches + 2 Pullman cars during the Victoria-Ramsgate winter service in 1954.

Above: 'Battle of Britain' 4-6-2 No 34066 *Spitfire* at Blacksole Summit after climbing the 1½ miles at 1 in 93 from Herne Bay. The 10-car 'Kentish Belle' usually loaded to about 420 tons gross during the summer working when this photograph was taken in 1956.

Centre right: Of the several classes of ex-L&SW locomotives working on the Kent Coast in the thirties, the rebuilt and superheated Drummond Class L12 were most frequently seen. (Originally these engines had water tube fireboxes and 8-wheeled tenders). No 424 was on an excursion train to Margate in 1938.

Bottom right: With a polished steel star embellishing the smokebox door, Class N1 No 1877 was working an up return excursion from Margate near Herne Bay in 1936.

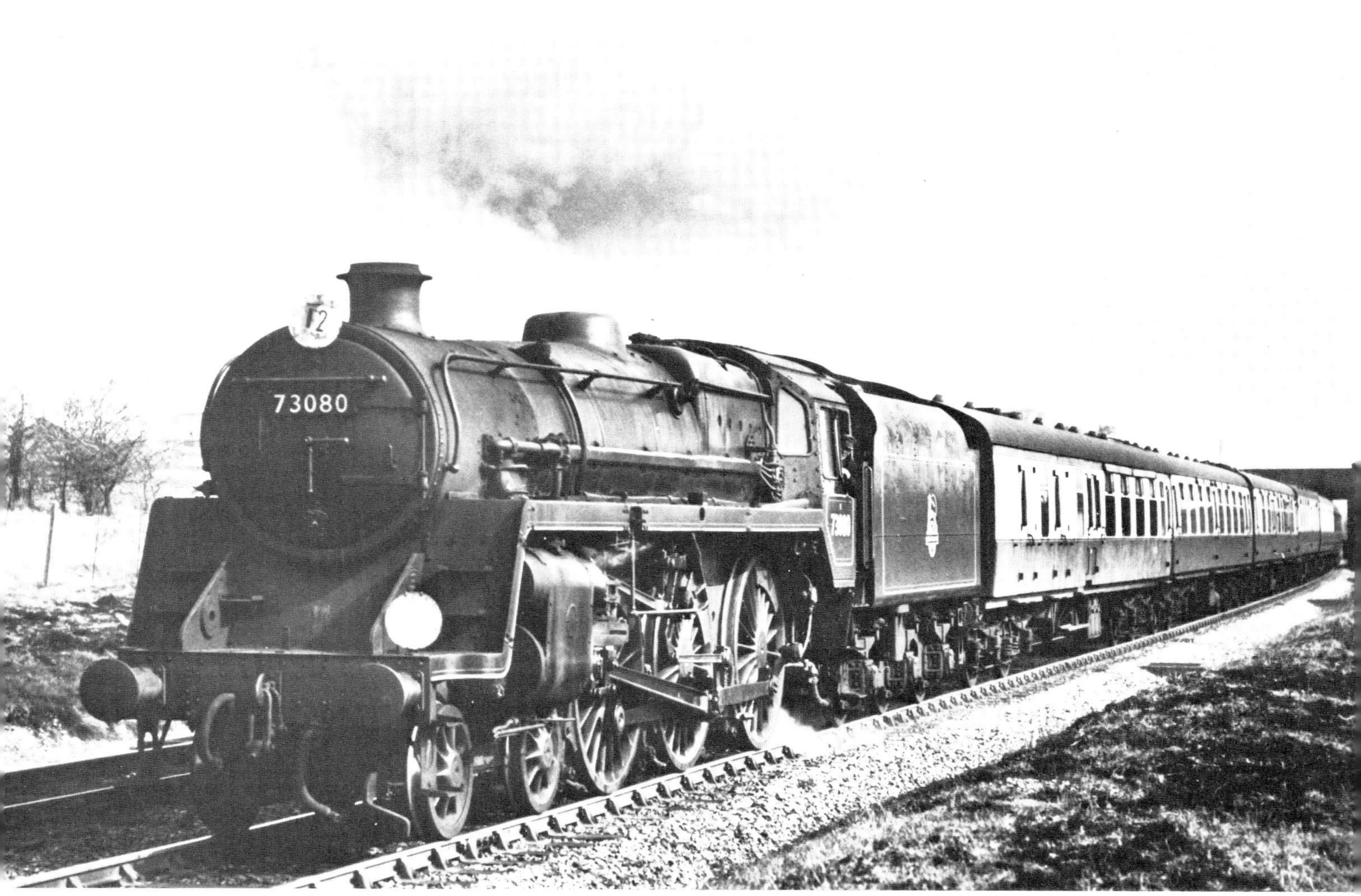
73080

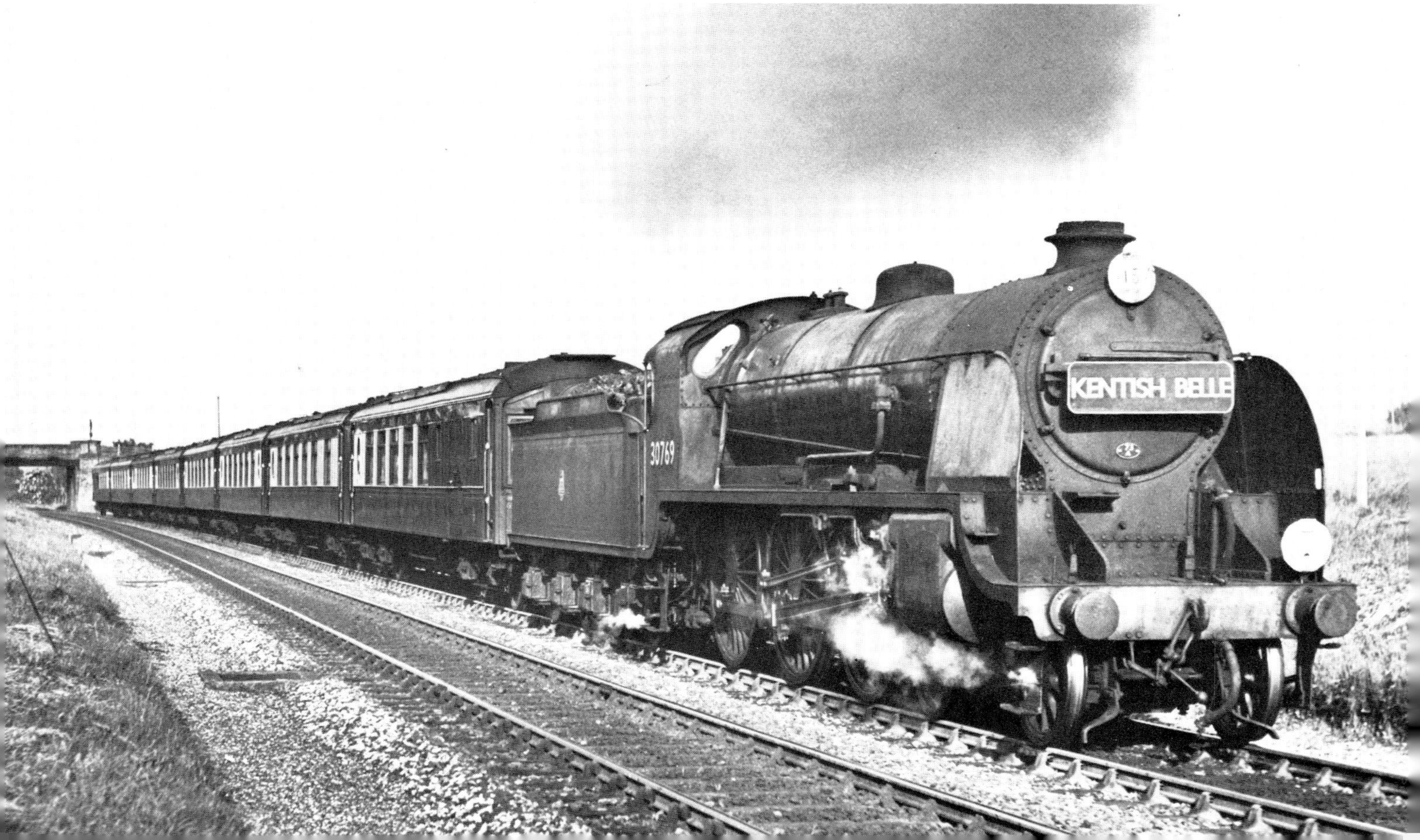
KENTISH BELLE
30769

Above left: Working a Ramsgate-Victoria fast train near Herne Bay in 1956, was Standard Class 5 4-6-0 No 73080.

Bottom left: Heading the up 'Kentish Belle' in 1953 was Class N15 No 30769 *Sir Balan*. The photograph was taken near Reculver.

Top: Heading the up 'Kentish Belle' across the Reculver Marshes in September 1956 was Class 4 No 75066.

Above: To save light engine movements, the locomotives of excursion trains terminating at Margate often worked forward to Ramsgate shed as pilots to regular trains. Seen here near Broadstairs in 1938 are Class T9 No 281, 'Schools' No 922 *Marlborough* and 'King Arthur' No 799 *Sir Ironside.*

Right: Up Kent Coast Pullman Car express leaving Margate in 1939. Class E1 No 1504.

Above: No 853 *Sir Richard Grenville* was 'running-in' on a 3-coach train of 'birdcage' stock leaving Ramsgate for Victoria in 1939.

Right: Ramsgate in 1955. A Class C 0-6-0 is at the carriage shed while Standard Class 4 No 75068 pulls away from the station with empty stock. Far right, is a Class U1 2-6-0 on a van train for Deal and Dover.

Below right: Dover Priory to Faversham slow train near Canterbury East in 1951. Class L 4-4-0 No 31780.

Left: Class 73/1 electro-diesel Bo-Bo No 73.110 pulling away from Snowdown Colliery with a long train of coal for Dover. (The headcode 2D is for trains working between Sheerness and Ashford via Canterbury East).

Below: No 31268, an SE&C Class C 0-6-0, leaving Adisham with a Faversham-Dover train in 1959.

Right: A slow train from Dover Priory to Faversham leaving Lydden in 1958. In charge was ex-LMS 2-6-2T No 41312. A number of these useful little tank engines came to the Southern. They were designed by Ivatt and known on the LMS as the 'Mickey Mouses'.

Below: Train of oil tank wagons leaving the Grain oil refinery in charge of Birmingham/Sulzer Bo-Bo diesel-electric No D6538 (later Class 33/1 No 33.118).

The Channel Ports in Kent

The old SE main line comes to Dover via Tonbridge and Ashford and, at Folkestone Junction, the Folkestone Harbour branch leaves it to descend for about a mile on a gradient of 1 in 30 to the Harbour station. For many years this branch was the province of the Stirling domeless Class R 0-6-0Ts of 1888 vintage which later were given domed boilers and became Class R1. These little engines also worked the Canterbury and Whitstable line on which they had reduced boiler mountings and smaller cabs in order to negotiate Tyler Hill Tunnel. There was considerable interchange of boilers between engines of the class so it was not unusual to see C&W engines at Folkestone or engines with small cabs and 'normal' boiler mountings and vice versa.

The heaviest boat trains from Folkestone Harbour often required three engines at the head-end with one and sometimes two, providing banking assistance. The sparks flew and the exhausts roared as, with regulators wide open and in full forward gear, they charged up the bank to the Junction. In 1930 a Class Z three-cylinder 0-8-0T was on trial. It was at least the equal of the two R1s but was too heavy for the Harbour bridge and so did not stay long. Then, in 1959 after 70 years of service, the old South Eastern engines were withdrawn and were replaced by Great Western 0-6-0PTs of the 46XX Series from South Wales. I made several footplate trips on these engines which usually were 'two in front and one behind' — I never saw them triple-headed. It was still a noisy and exciting ride though somehow one never got quite the thrill and yes, the fun, of riding the old R1s.

Now, of course, all boat trains are composed of multiple-unit electric stock. There is little noise, no fuss and few problems.

Dover is the busiest passenger port in the world — in 1977 no fewer than 7.8million travellers passed through the port. Since it was decided not to build the Channel Tunnel, it has been rapidly developed and enlarged in order to provide better facilities, not only for passengers but also for the increasing volume of freight traffic. At the busy and thriving Eastern Docks, all freight and passenger traffic arrives by road and all the ferries regularly using these docks are passenger car ferries or RoRo (Roll-on Roll Off) ships taking freight vehicles only.

At the Western Docks, the railway is much in evidence. The Marine station was opened in 1915 having been built on reclaimed land adjoining the western wall of the Admiralty Pier. Before electrification of the railway (in 1959 via Dover Priory and 1961 via Ashford) there were one terminal and three through roads, the latter leading far out on to the pier for shunting and marshalling boat trains and for engine release purposes. Now two tracks extend only as far as is necessary to allow a 4-car mu to be switched from one centre track to another while the third track extension is adequate for engine release only. Trains from the old South Eastern main line via Ashford enter the station from the west after running along the foot of the cliffs and, in the steam era, passing the locomotive sheds on the seaward side of the line. Trains over the former LC&D line via Faversham, Canterbury and Dover Priory come in from a northerly direction.

Ships berthing alongside the Marine station are usually conventional passenger ferries. Four such ships belonging to Belgian Marine are still in service but the only British ship of this type is the twin-screw turbine steamer *Caesarea* which also works from Folkestone and which came to Kent from Weymouth where she was employed on the Channel Islands service. At the seaward end of the Marine station there is now a link-span to serve the car ferries.

An important feature of the Western Docks is the Train Ferry Terminal. After many constructional problems the dock was finally completed in 1936. Access over the link-span to the train ferry ship must always be level and so the water in the dock cannot be tidal and a single gate is provided to maintain it at the correct level. Powerful rotary pumps enable ships to enter at any state of the tide and the gate is hinged to lie flat on the seabed when ships are passing into or out of the dock.

Approach lines to the Train Ferry Dock are not electrified and the ferries, each of which has four rail tracks, are loaded and off-loaded by diesel shunters working side by side on adjacent approach roads. By this method the ship is kept on an even keel, the need to use her equalising tanks is avoided and time is saved. During the days of steam, a single locomotive, usually a Class C 0-6-0 was used and, as one side of the ship had to be loaded at a time, the ship could list several degrees and the equalising tanks were needed to correct this.

The train ferry service is between Dover and Dunkirk. It carries a lot of rail freight and as many private and commercial road vehicles as can be accommodated in the space available in the ship. The only passenger service is the 'Night Ferry' which, composed of special Wagon-lits sleeping cars (built to British loading gauge) runs between London (Victoria), Lille and Paris (Nord). One car is detached at Lille for Brussels. I have photographed the train only once as, outward it arrives at Dover at 23.40 and inwards at 06.05 and I very much dislike getting up early though I have 'footplated' both the up and the down trains with steam and with electric locomotives.

One of Britain's most famous trains went into service on 15 May 1929. This was the all-Pullman 'Golden Arrow' which, hauled by a 'Lord Nelson' class locomotive, left Victoria at 11.00 for Dover. On arrival there passengers were transferred immediately to the Southern Railway's SS *Canterbury* which had been built by Denny of Dumbarton specially for the service. At Calais the Pullman train 'Flèche d'Or' was drawn up at the Gare Maritime and, in charge of a Nord 4-cylinder compound Super-Pacific, was soon on its way to Paris and (usually) a punctual 17.35 arrival. The return train left the Gare du Nord at 12.00 noon and the arrival time in London was 18.35. This was a 'limited service' every passenger being allocated a seat and a supplementary fare was charged.

The service was, of course, suspended during the war years and *Canterbury* became a Landing Ship Infantry (LSI). She survived and after the war was completely refitted and was ready for the resumption of the 'Golden Arrow' service on 15 April 1946. She did not remain long on the service for, seven months later, she was replaced by a new and much larger ship. This was SS *Invicta* which had been laid down in 1939 and, on completion, in 1940, had become an

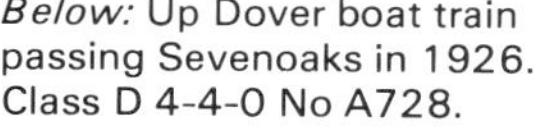

Below: Up Dover boat train passing Sevenoaks in 1926. Class D 4-4-0 No A728.

assault ship. But no longer was this ship reserved solely for 'Golden Arrow' passengers as she carried also those who had arrived by ordinary boat train half an hour earlier.

In England, Bulleid's Pacifics of both the 'Merchant Navy' and 'West Country' classes worked the train while the 'Flèche d'Or' was headed by a 4-cylinder compound Chapelon Pacific of Series 231 E. Late in 1951, after being on exhibition at the Festival of Britain, British Railways Class 7 Pacific No 70004 *William Shakespeare*, kept in immaculate condition, was used exclusively on the down and up 'Golden Arrow'. On 'shed days' her stand-in was No 70014 *Iron Duke.* During this period one of the Southern's three 1-Co-Co-1 diesel-electric locomotives was tried out on the train.

In September 1952 the down 'Golden Arrow' was retimed to leave Victoria at 14.00, and was routed via Folkestone. The channel crossing was made in the new French ship SS *Cote d'Azur* which, with a speed of 25.5kts was the fastest of all the cross-channel ships. The ship and the 'Flèche d'Or' carried not only the Pullman passengers but also those from the preceding ordinary service. The return service was via Dover so the locomotive, after being turned at Folkestone Junction, hauled the empty stock tender-first from there to Dover Marine.

In 1957, *William Shakespeare* left the Southern and Bulleid Pacifics again took over the working, this being among the first duties for these engines as rebuilt. Then in 1960 the down train reverted to its original departure time and Dover again became the port of embarkation.

In France, the Paris-Amiens-Lille line was electrified in 1960 and the 'Flèche d'Or was therefore worked by steam, only between Amiens and Calais. In 1967, the Chapelon Pacifics were withdrawn and their duties were taken over by the ex-PLM Pacifics of Series 231 G and 231 K until in their turn, they were displaced by diesel-electric locomotives in January 1969.

Returning to Britain, electrification of the main line to Dover Marine was completed in 1961 and the Southern Bo-Bo electric locomotives took over the working of both the 'Golden Arrow' and the 'Night Ferry', all other regular boat trains being composed of electric multiple-unit stock. With increasing competition from the airlines, luxury travel by rail and sea gradually became less popular, and it was said, the 'Golden Arrow' service was maintained only at the request of the French who were reluctant to lose one of their prestige trains. The service was withdrawn on 30 September 1972. An era ended: a little bit of railway glamour was lost.

Below: Down boat train for Dover Marine passing Herne Hill in 1928. No A767 *Sir Valence* at the head-end was still without smoke deflectors.

35001
21

Above left: No 35001 *Channel Packet*, pouring forth black smoke, was approaching Ashford under clear signals at the head of a down boat train in 1958.

Left: A lucky shot near Marden in 1959 when two Dover boat trains, each travelling at high speed, were about to pass each other. The down (left) was headed by No 34083, *605 Squadron*, while No 34070 *Manston* was in charge of the up train.

Above: Up continental boat express near Sandling in 1957. No 34070 *Manston*, 'Battle of Britain' class.

Right: With their traction motors powered by batteries these two motor baggage vans are seen approaching the quayside over non-electrified track at Dover Marine.

Top right: MV *Prinses Maria-Esmeralda* (5635, '75) is one of the latest Belgian car ferries to join the Sealink fleet between Dover and Ostend. These ships have largely replaced the conventional passenger ferries in the Belgian fleet and they operate from the Western Docks by the Marine station as well as from the Eastern Docks.

Centre right: The French MV Chartres (4565, '73) is a dual-purpose ferry ship with four rail tracks which are loaded through the stern door. She also has a lifting bow and when in use as a car ferry (as here) she can load through either the bow or the stern. She is seen approaching the link span at Folkestone.

Below: Up boat train leaving Folkestone Junction in 1957. The locomotive is No 34005 *Barnstaple* a rebuilt 'West Country'.

Above: Lord Nelson No 850 leaving Dover Marine with the up 'Golden Arrow' in 1935.

Left: The original ship built for the 'Golden Arrow' service in 1929 was the twin-screw turbine SS *Canterbury* (2910, '29) here seen bound for Dover in 1930.

GOLDEN
ARROW
21C134

Above left: In the days of steam the 'Golden Arrow' was usually banked out of Victoria up the 1 in 62 to Grosvenor Bridge. Here Class C No 31578 is seen providing the 'push'.

Left: Leaving Shakespeare Cliff Tunnel on the approach to Dover Marine, No 21C134 (un-named) was working the 'Golden Arrow' in 1948.

Above: 'Golden Arrow' arriving at Dover Marine in 1947. No 21C119 (un-named) was in charge.

Right: The twin-screw turbine SS *Invicta* (4191, '40) which replaced *Canterbury* on the service after the war.

GOLDEN
ARROW

GOLDEN
ARROW

Left: No 70014 *Iron Duke* was deputising for *William Shakespeare* on the up 'Golden Arrow' passing Dover shed in 1956. Seen 'on shed' are Brighton 'Terrier' No 32636, a Class L and a 'King Arthur'.

Below left: Passing Shorncliffe on a wet evening in 1961. No 34100 *Appledore* was working the up 'Golden Arrow'.

Right: Class N No 31848 was heading an up pw train when photographed from No 34005 *Barnstaple* on the down 'Golden Arrow' in 1957.

Below: The down 'Golden Arrow', in charge of No 34100 *Appledore*, was photographed near Smeeth in 1960.

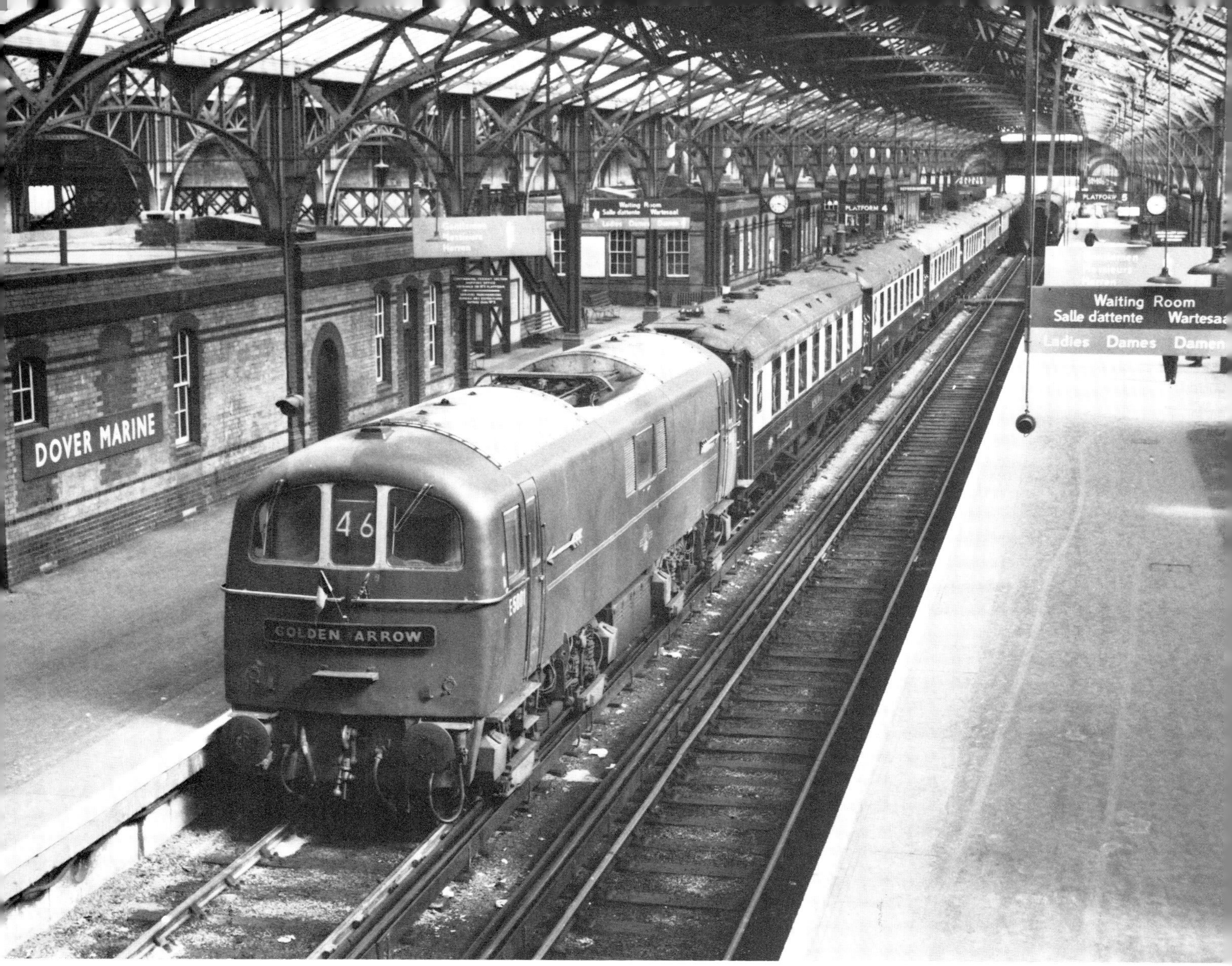

DOVER MARINE
46
GOLDEN ARROW
Waiting Room
Salle d'attente Wartesaa
Ladies Dames Damen

Above left: Southern Bo-Bo electric locomotive No E5001 (later Class 71) on the up 'Golden Arrow' at Dover Marine in 1963.

Left: In France, the 'Golden Arrow' continued its journey to Paris as the 'Flèche d'Or'. In pre-war days until 1937 it was worked by the famous Nord Super Pacifics of which No 231 C 36 is seen here with a Boulogne-Paris train passing La Chapelle in 1951.

Top: For two years before World War II and after the war, Chapelon engines of Series 231 E were the regular engines for the 'Flèche d'Or'. No 231 E 16 was pulling away from the Gare Maritime Calais, when photographed in 1947.

Above: With a gross load of about 625 tonnes behind the tender, ex-PLM Pacific No 231 G 87 was approaching Caffiers Summit with the southbound 'Flèche d'Or' in 1968. Note the clear exhaust!

Right: In 1961, a strike caused the cancellation of the regular 'Flèche d'Or'. A substitute service was operated composed of secondary stock and hauled from Paris by mixed traffic locomotive No BB 16022.

Far left, top: Class R1 0-6-0Ts Nos 31154 and 31069 (with C&W cab) leaving Folkestone Harbour with empty 'Golden Arrow' stock in 1952. At the Junction station the empty train was worked to Dover Marine to form the up train on arrival of *Invicta* from Calais.

Far left, bottom: Working the empty 'Golden Arrow' stock from Folkestone Harbour up to the Junction in 1959 were ex-GW pannier tanks Nos 4616 and 4631.

Left: The twin screw SS *Cote d'Azur* (3998, '51) was owned by SNCF and it carried 'Golden Arrow' passengers from Folkestone to Calais from 1952 until 1960.

Below: 'Merchant Navy' class Pacific No 35015 *Rotterdam Lloyd* at Folkestone Junction awaiting the arrival of the up 'Golden Arrow' from Folkestone Harbour in 1959.

Above left: One of the original three train-ferry ships on the Dover-Dunkirk service was SS *Shepperton Ferry* (2839, '35) seen here leaving Dover in 1937.

Left: Class C 0-6-0 No 31243 loading *Twickenham Ferry* at Dover in 1954.

Above: The Dover train-ferry dock showing the gate being lowered to allow the French ferry, MV *Saint-Germain* (3094, '51) to leave.

Centre right: Class 08 0-6-0 diesel-electric shunters Nos 08.833 and 08.830 working side by side while off-loading freight vans from the train ferry *Saint-Germain* at Dover in 1977.

Bottom right: Approaching Dover, the latest British train ferry is the MV *Vortigern.*

Right: MV *Saint Eloi* (4500, '72) was the latest French train ferry and was owned by ALA (Angleterre-Lorraine-Alsace). She has, however, now been transferred to British ownership.

Below: Up 'Night Ferry' near Faversham in 1954. 4-4-0 Class L1 No 31758 piloting a 3-cylinder 'Battle of Britain' class 4-6-2.

Kentish Private Railways

The development of the Kent coalfield in the early years of this century resulted in the promotion, in 1910, of a railway to connect some of the collieries with the SE&C main line. In 1911 the East Kent Railway was opened between Shepherd's Well and Tilmanstone Colliery a distance of 2¼ miles but which involved the boring of the 585 yards of Golgotha Tunnel. In 1912 the line had reached Wingham eight miles on, but some projected coal workings were abandoned and not until 1925 did the railway start an extension towards Canterbury. But the money ran out and the railway ended in a field.

During World War I the old Roman port of Richborough became a relief port for Dover and the EKR built a line from Eastry to serve it. But after the war the port was closed and the railway lost heavily as a result.

The fortunes of the East Kent dwindled until World War II brought another increase in traffic but, once again, when the war was over, traffic fell off and, by the time the line was nationalised in 1948, it was in poor shape. In 1951 the railway was closed except for the Shepherd's Well-Tilmanstone Colliery section which still operates.

The Engineer for the East Kent Railway, Lieutenant-Colonel H. F. Stephens, was adept at obtaining old locomotives, repairing and maintaining them to a standard adequate for light railway duties. The locomotive shed at Shepherd's Well usually contained an assortment of locomotives the origins of which were, to say the least, unfamiliar, such as the Whitland & Cardigan, the Weston, Clevedon & Portishead, the Rother Valley and the Richborough Port Railways. In addition were 'relics' from the L&SW and the SE&C.

L. T. C. Rolt once wrote a delightful book entitled *Lines of Character.* The East Kent certainly qualified for such a description as indeed did another of the Colonel Stephens railways — the Kent & East Sussex. As the Rother Valley Railway it was opened in 1900 to connect Tenterden with the SE&C Tonbridge-Hastings line at Robertsbridge. The original Tenterden station was that which is now known as Rolvenden, the mile-long extension up a gradient of 1 in 50 to Tenterden Town being opened in 1903. In 1904, the railway changed its name to the Kent & East Sussex and the following year, was extended northwards to Headcorn on the SE&C main line to Dover and 21½ miles from Robertsbridge.

The locomotives of the K&ES were not all in the 'Colonel Stephens tradition' for two 2-4-0Ts were purchased from Hawthorn Leslie in 1899 and a powerful 0-8-0T from the same builders in 1904. For the rest, there were two LB&SC 'Terrier' tanks, two L&SW 0-6-0s of 1873 vintage and an 0-6-0ST built in 1876 for the North Pembroke & Fishguard Railway. The K&ES also owned two petrol railcars converted from 'buses.

From its opening until the end of World War I the railway was fairly successful but, from 1924 until the start of World War II it was often in financial trouble. Taken over by Government in 1939 its future was assured until the end of hostilities and it then managed to keep going until nationalised in 1948. For a time it seemed that the railway could be retained as a useful connecting freight line between the Hastings and Dover lines. Much of the track was relaid and the locomotive stock modernised. But things did not turn out well and the railway was closed to traffic in 1961.

But the K&ES did not die — at least, not all of it for, after overcoming many problems, enthusiasts formed the Tenterden Railway Company in 1971 with the object of running passenger trains between Tenderden Town and Bodiam. In February 1974 the railway began operating as far as Wittersham Road, four miles from Tenterden. The remaining six miles to Bodiam is for the future.

There are two interesting narrow-gauge steam railways in Kent which are a 'must' for all who roam the Southern rails. The first of these the 2ft 6in gauge Sittingbourne & Kemsley Light Railway was, until 1969, an industrial line which, since 1908 connected the Bowater Paper Mill at Sittingbourne first with the Company's dock at Milton Creek and later with the much larger Ridham Dock and with the new mill at Kemsley.

In 1969, when road transport replaced the rail services, Bowaters were reluctant to scrap the railway and the 2½ mile section between Sittingbourne and Kemsley together with rolling stock and six locomotives were presented to the Locomotive Club of Great Britain. The railway is now the property of an independent company.

Operating nearly 14 route miles of track between Hythe and Dungeness is the 15in gauge Romney Hythe & Dymchurch Railway. The first 8½ miles from Hythe to New Romney were opened in 1927 and are double-track. The remaining section to Dungeness is now single track and is mostly laid on shingle. Operation of the line follows full scale practice with colour-light signalling and single line tablet for the New Romney-Dungeness section.

The railway serves many holiday camps and chalets and passes through some of the most pleasant parts of the Romney Marshes. One of the most important assignments ever given to the RH&D is to provide a regular school train between Burmarsh Road and New Romney all the year round. A 16-coach train is required with a Pacific locomotive at each end. The railway provides reliability and punctuality and replaces a bus service which provided neither.

At Dungeness interest is always aroused by the two lighthouses and by the huge pile of the nuclear power stations. New Romney is the headquarters of the railway. Here there is a large engine shed, workshops, carriage shops, a museum and a fine model railway as well as excellent refreshment rooms.

The RH&D steam locomotives not only look like the real thing, they sound and smell the same as did their main line prototypes when steam ruled at Kings Cross! Ever since I first made their acquaintance nearly 50 years ago, I never cease to be fascinated and thrilled by these beautiful machines and one of my most cherished memories is of the short period I spent as a relief engine driver on the railway.

Below: Kent & East Sussex Railway 0-6-0ST No 8 with burnished brass dome and safety valve bonnet was photographed at Tenterden in 1937. It was built in 1876 for the North Pembroke & Fishguard Railway and was then named *Ringing Rock.*

Top right: Southern Railway Class 01 0-6-0 No 1390 was on loan to the K&ES when it was photographed with a train from Headcorn to Tenterden in 1947.

Bottom right: K&ES Tenterden Town station in 1977 with a train for Wittersham Road headed by No 23, Hunslet 0-6-0T.

TENTERDEN TOWN
Nº 23

Above: Another shot of K&ES 0-6-0ST No 23, this time hard at work with a train from Wittersham Road on the 1 in 50 incline from Rolvenden up to Tenterden Town.

Top right: An unusual acquisition by the K&ES was this 2-6-0 No 19 which came from the Norwegian State Railways on which it was No 376 of Class 21C. The locomotive is seen standing outside the new repair shops at Rolvenden.

Right: K&ES No 10 0-4-0T *Gervase*, a most interesting conversion of a Manning Wardle saddle tank to a Sentinal chain-driven locomotive with a vertical engine and boiler.

Nº 19
K&ESR

K & ESR
GERVASE
10
Nº

Above: East Kent Railway: ex-SE&C Class 01 0-6-0 No 2 with a mixed train at Canterbury Road (Wingham) terminus in 1947. The coach next to the locomotive is an ex-L&SW 3rd brake composite.

Right: East Kent Railway: An elderly countrywoman with her shopping was the only passenger to alight at Knowlton Halt. Note the cattle grid.

Below right: Heading a train of coal empties from Shepherd's Well to Tilmanstone Colliery near Eythorne in 1977, was Class 09 0-6-0 diesel-electric Shunter No 09.018.

Above: One of the last fireless steam locomotives in the country was this 0-4-0 built in 1956 by Andrew Barclay at Kilmarnock and, in 1976, working at the Imperial Paper Mills at Gravesend.

Above left: Bowaters' *Melior* 0-4-2ST (Kerr Stuart 1924) has Hackworth valve gear. Seen here working a train of empty pulp wagons at Sittingbourne.

Left: Triumph 0-6-2T (Bagnall 1934) arriving at Sittingbourne with a train of wood pulp from Kemsley, on Bowaters' railway.

Above: Monarch, double bogie 4-cylinder 0-4-4-0T was one of three such engines built by Bagnall in 1953. Two went to Natal to work on the 2ft 0 in gauge railways in sugar estates, while the third came to the 2ft 6in gauge Bowaters' line. The engines were not compounds.

Centre right: The road ahead as seen from S&KLR *Premier.*

Bottom right: Premier 0-4-2ST (Kerr Stuart 1908) with an S&KLR train between Kemsley and Sittingbourne.

R H D R
10

Left: A busy scene at the Hythe terminus of the RH&D: 4-6-2 No 2 *Northern Chief* leaving for Dungeness; No 10 *Doctor Syn* another 4-6-2 on the engine release road and 4-8-2 No 5 *Hercules* on the right, with a train for New Romney.

Centre left: In 1969 this special RH&D train ran non-stop from Hythe to Dungeness and back to Hythe covering the 28 miles in 81 minutes. The two 'Canadian' Pacifics No 10 *Doctor Syn* and No 9 *Winston Churchill* were at the head-end. The train is seen crossing the shingle near The Pilot.

Bottom left: RH&D Hythe to New Romney Train crossing Botolph's Bridge hauled by No 11 *Black Prince*

Right: RH&D No 5 *Hercules* was generously polluting the atmosphere for my photographic benefit as it crossed the Duke of York's Bridge en route for New Romney. This bridge was replaced in 1968 by a simple structure comprising four rolled steel joists on which are laid standard gauge wood sleepers supporting the rails.

Below: The RH&D owns several locomotives powered by internal combustion engines. Here is No 3 *Red Gauntlet*, a petrol engined 0-4-0 working a permanent way train at New Romney.

Above right: RH&D New Romney station in 1977 with *The Bug* on a special train alongside No 3 *Southern Maid.*

Right: RH&D: the footplate of *The Bug.*

Below: RH&D: the 'works' of 4-6-2 *Doctor Syn* show the elegance of the design and its very close approximation to full size practice.

London Brighton & South Coast: Central Division

The London Brighton & South Coast Railway formed the smallest of the three divisions of the Southern Railway. Its main line from London Bridge to Brighton was only 50½ miles in length and, in view of the very considerable commuter traffic it has often been referred to as an 'outer suburban railway'. But with its South Coast line extending from Hastings to Portsmouth and its network of lines in Sussex, the LB&SC was much more than that. At a time when it was quite usual for employees to show respect and loyalty to their companies, Brighton men showed not only respect but pride and real affection. Even the passengers loved their railway though my memory of the Brighton passenger trains is that they were rather uncomfortable and often ran late. It was probably due to the small size and compactness of the railway that everybody seemed to know, or know of, everybody else. Even after the 1923 Grouping the 'atmosphere' of the Brighton line was still distinctive.

My acquaintance with the LB&SC began in 1912 when I spent a month with my grandparents in South Croydon — the first of several visits. The garden of their house was separated from the main line by only a high iron fence through which one could get one's head stuck when trying to see further down the line! How I regret that in those days I had no camera! My grandfather was well-known and much respected in the area and through his influence I was allowed on locomotive footplates and even into a signal box. On returning home to Worksop from these visits I found that my deeply-rooted affection for 'our own Great Central' had at least found a distant rival!

I suppose much of the glamour of the Brighton was due to the undoubted elegance and beauty of its locomotives and I can still recall the wonderment I felt on first seeing those immaculate 'yellow engines' with their shining brass and copper adornments. As I got older, I was able to appreciate more fully their elegance and symmetry of design although none of them could ever exceed the beauty of the Great Central Atlantics.

The Brighton was mainly a 'tank engine line' and with its extensive suburban system this was sound policy though much of the main line work was also performed very satisfactorily by 4-4-2, 4-6-2 and 4-6-4 tank locomotives. Which reminds me that when the handsome 4-6-4T engines were found to be unsteady at high speeds they were rebuilt with well tanks between the frames. In order not to detract from their fine appearance, the side tank sheeting was retained. Even in locomotives it appears that sometimes beauty is only skin deep! The smallest tank engines were the 0-6-0 'Terriers', some of which still survive. Even in my young days I used to wonder at the heavy suburban trains these little engines were, at times, called upon to handle. No wonder Brighton punctuality was not always as good as it ought to have been.

The most powerful passenger tender engines were the Marsh Atlantics which were, of course, almost Great Northern, for Marsh had been Ivatt's Chief Assistant at Doncaster before he went to Brighton. But it was astonishing how the Brighton chimney and a larger cab could make his engines look so different.

The LB&SC had two London termini: it owned part of Victoria usually referred to as 'the Brighton side' to distinguish it from the other part of the station, 'the Chatham side' and it had its own terminal station at London Bridge alongside and at a slightly lower level than the South Eastern 'through' station. From Victoria, the climb to Grosvenor Bridge presented the same problems to Brighton locomotives as it did to those of the Chatham but, after crossing the bridge, Brighton trains bear off to the right and on a falling gradient join and run parallel to the London & South Western main line from Waterloo. After passing Clapham Junction, the lines diverge, the Brighton going off left towards Wandsworth Common. The line from London Bridge is joined at Windmill

Bridge Junction, north of East Croydon. The old Brighton main line went through Redhill, the Coulsdon-Redhill section being owned jointly with the South Eastern (and then the SE&C). Not surprisingly, the heavy traffic over this section caused many delays so a new line was built and opened in 1900. This was the so-called 'Quarry Line' which leaves the old joint line at Coulsdon North and, by-passing Redhill, joins it again 6½ miles further south at Earlswood. From there, on mainly gently falling gradients, the main line is routed through Gatwick, Three Bridges and Haywards Heath to Preston Park and Brighton. At Keymer Junction, 9¾ miles from Brighton the line for Lewes and Eastbourne goes off in a south-easterly direction.

In addition to its main line, the LB&SC had three other lines running roughly north and south which, with some cross-country links, served some of the wealthiest residential areas in England. In order to provide more comfortable travel for its wealthy commuters, the first Pullman car was put into service between London and Brighton in 1875 and others soon followed. Electric lighting was a feature of these cars, first supplied by batteries but soon by dynamo belt-driven from the axle.

By 1847, a branch line from Southerham Junction (Lewes) to Newhaven at the mouth of the River Ouse had been completed and, in collaboration with the French Chemin de Fer de l'Ouest, the LB&SC began a cross-channel service to Dieppe. The South Eastern Railway, however, raised legal objections and for the next 20 years the service was carried on by (in name) an independent company. Sealink car

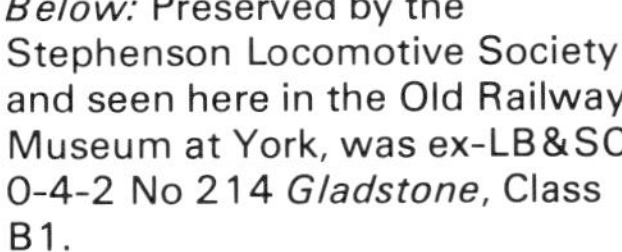

Below: Preserved by the Stephenson Locomotive Society and seen here in the Old Railway Museum at York, was ex-LB&SC 0-4-2 No 214 *Gladstone*, Class B1.

ferries now operate regularly between Newhaven and Dieppe.

In 1911 discussions between the LB&SC and the Chemin de Fer de l'Etat (successor to the Ouest) started with a view to the introduction of a train ferry service to Dieppe. Had it not been for the outbreak of World War I Newhaven would probably have become Britain's first cross-channel train ferry terminal.

Largely as a result of competition from the LCC electric tramways system the LB&SC were in the forefront of railway electrification in Britain. In 1909 suburban electrification was started and a quite extensive system developed using single-phase, alternating current at 6,700V at a frequency of 25 cycles per second. Current collection was from overhead catenary. For various reasons, the Southern Railway adopted the third rail direct current system as standard and, in 1933, the Brighton was the first main line to be electrified.

The LB&SC line between East Grinstead and Lewes was closed to traffic in March 1958. Two years later, the five-mile section between Horsted Keynes and Sheffield Park was reopened by the Bluebell Railway Preservation Society and this enterprising project has been very successful. The line is operated under the regulations governing Light Railways and a train service runs at weekends throughout the year and daily during the summer. The railway owns 14 locomotives ranging in size from a 'West Country' Pacific to an Aveling & Porter rail traction engine. The five-mile journey is not only picturesque but interesting from a railway point of view with a considerable incline against northbound trains.

Below: Approaches to London Bridge stations. Left foreground: the ex-South Eastern 'through' station. Right foreground: the ex-LB&SC terminal.

Above: Before electrification in 1933, the 'King Arthurs' with 6-wheel tenders did much of the main line work on the Brighton. Approaching Earlswood with an up slow train in 1927 was No E799 *Sir Ironside.*

Right: Hurrying past Earlswood with the down 'Southern Belle' in 1927 was 4-6-4T No B333 *Remembrance* of Class L.

Below right: Class N15X No 2333 *Remembrance* seen here in 1936 at Nine Elms, was rebuilt from the LB&SC 4-6-4T which carried the same name. (See above).

Right: Brighton Atlantic No 32424 *Beachy Head* passing Burgess Hill with an up special Pullman train in 1952. This train, one of two run to celebrate Brighton Works Centenary, easily maintained the 1hr schedule between Victoria and Brighton in each direction.

Below: The down Brighton Sunday Pullman near Balcombe in 1926. This heavy train of eight clerestory-roofed Pullmans and a bogie van was headed by Class I3 4-4-2T No B90 fitted with a Weir feed-water pump.

Top right: Ex-Southern Co-Co electric locomotive No 20002 on a southbound freight passing Three Bridges in 1962.

Centre right: Entering Three Bridges in 1947 with a pick-up freight from Horsham was Class C2x No 2445.

Below: Class 33/2 Bo-Bo diesel-electric No 33.202 with a train of empty bogie hoppers at Redhill.

Far right, top: Hurrying through Clapham Junction with a Victoria to Tunbridge Wells train in 1960 was BR Class 4 No 75069 with double exhaust.

Far right, bottom: Working a Brighton-Oxted-London Bridge train near Ashurst in 1950 was a 4-6-2T No 32325 formally named *Abergavenny*. This Class J engine had Stephenson valve gear and a Weir feed pump.

Above: Heading a train composed of a four-wheeled van and a three-coach rake of ex-SE&C 'birdcage' stock was Class J 4-6-2T No 2326, formerly named *Bessborough.* The photograph was taken at Lewes in 1934.

Left: Up Eastbourne express composed of three 4-CIG units entering Lewes in 1976.

Above right: In July 1961, as a result of many complaints of late running, the important 18.10 train from Victoria to Tunbridge Wells was powered by a rebuilt 'Battle of Britain' class locomotive. No 34050 *Royal Observer Corps* heads the train out of Victoria.

Right: Diesel on trial. Diesel-electric Bo-Bo No 10800 (827hp) on loan from LMR working a train for the Oxted line from Victoria in 1951.

34050

Steam, Diesel and Electric at Hampden Park in 1962

Above: Rebuilt 'West Country' No 34100 *Appledore* on a Birmingham to Eastbourne express.

Right: Bo-Bo diesel-electric No D6592 (later Class 33/2 No 33.207) also on a Birmingham to Eastbourne express.

Below right: Victoria-Eastbourne-Hastings train headed by 6-PAN set introduced in 1933.

Left: Victoria-Tunbridge Wells train leaving Groombridge in 1947. Ex-LB&SC 4-4-2T No 2076 Class I3.

Below: Leaving Groombridge in 1959 with a Tonbridge to Victoria via East Grinstead train was ex-LM&SR 2-6-4T No 42103.

Above left: Leaving East Grinstead with a train for Three Bridges in 1951 was No 32520 Class E4.

Left: Ex-LM&SR 2-6-4T No 42092 on a train for Lewes and Brighton leaving East Grinstead in 1950.

Above: Dirty and run-down after hard work during World War II, Class K No 2339 was heading an up local freight near Dorking Town in 1947.

Centre right: Ex-LB&SC Class D3 0-4-4T No 2383 passing Hurst Green Junction box with a push-and-pull train for Oxted in 1938.

Bottom right: No 2077 a 4-4-2T of Class I3 slowly approaches Hurst Green Junction with a fast train for East Grinstead in 1938.

RCTS
32636
RCTS
S^PL
32636

2039

Above left: 'Terrier' No 32636 formerly No 72 *Fenchurch* working a special train from Kemp Town entering Brighton in 1952.

Left: Rebuilt with sleeve valve cylinders as a 'guinea pig' for Bulleid's 'Leader' class, No 2039 *Hartland Point* was photographed in 1948 at Uckfield while working a test train.

Above: Class D1 0-4-2T No 2221 was heading a train of 'birdcage' stock at Tunbridge Wells West in 1936.

Right: Tunbridge Wells to East Grinstead train near High Rocks in 1947. Class D3 0-4-4T No 2390 with Ashford safety valves.

Above: The bold appearance of the rebuilt Brighton 4-4-0s of Class B4x is shown to advantage in this shot of No 2050 at Oxted in 1938.

Right: French cross-channel passenger steamship *Arromanches* (2600, '46) leaving Newhaven for Dieppe in 1961.

Below right: French (Sealink) car ferry *Villandry* (3444, '64) with bow and stern doors arriving at Newhaven in 1978. The ship is swinging and will secure stern-on to the link-span seen on the left of the view.

Left: Bluebell Railway: Ex-LB&SC 'Terrier' No 55 *Stepney* at Horsted Keynes.

Below: Beautifully restored by the Bluebell engineers, 'West Country' Pacific No 21C123 *Blackmore Vale* backs past Horsted Keynes South box.

Top right: Contrasts in preservation are evident in the Bluebell Railway: Aveling & Porter rail traction engine and . . .

Centre right: . . . The ex-GWR 'Earl' class No 3217 (which never carried its intended name *Earl of Berkeley*).

Below: Bluebell Railway: Horsted Keynes station with Class H No 263 running round its train.

Far right, top: Bluebell Railway: 'West Country' No 21C123 *Blackmore Vale* with a train from Sheffield Park to Horsted Keynes.

Far right, bottom: Bluebell Railway: Ex-SE&C Class C 0-6-0 and H 0-4-4T double heading a train for Horsted Keynes leaving Sheffield Park.

SOUTHERN
21C123

3
SE & CR

Right: Bluebell Railway: Class H No 263 drifts gently down to Sheffield Park with a train from Horsted Keynes.

Below: Bluebell Railway's new locomotive shop at Sheffield Park. Seen left is ex-L&SW Adams 4-4-2T No 488 which was sold in 1917 to the Ministry of Munitions. In 1919 it went to the East Kent Railway as their No 5 but in 1946 was purchased by the Southern who repaired it for use on their Lyme Regis branch. It was renumbered 30583 by BR and, in 1961 was purchased by the Bluebell Railway.

The Isle of Wight

I always regret not having visited the Isle of Wight before 1947 by which time all the highly individual locomotives which ran the three independent railways on the Island had been withdrawn. At the time of my first visit nearly all trains were in charge of the little Adams 0-4-4Ts of L&SW Class 02 though one or two ex- LB&SC 0-6-0Ts were still at work.

On my most recent visit to the Island, apart from a short preservation line operating between Haven Street and Wootton on the former Ryde-Newport line, there was no steam and very little railway. In fact, only the 8½ miles between Ryde Pier Head and Shanklin are in use. Furthermore, this is now an electrified line and the trains are made up of ex-London Transport tube stock. On one of my visits there was even a Cockney railwayman admonishing us to 'Maind the doors'.

There are three official ways of travelling to the Island: from Portsmouth to Ryde — this was formerly an LB&SC/L&SW joint service; from Lymington to Yarmouth — the L&SW route and from Southampton to Cowes. This last is operated by the 'Red Funnel Line' ships. There are car ferries on all routes but Sealink has three handsome conventional passenger ferries which run between Portsmouth and Ryde. All the paddle steamers have now been withdrawn.

Below: Ryde to Newport train near Smallbrook in 1950. Ex-L&SW Class 02 No 27 *Merstone.*

SOUTHERN
CARISBROOKE
13

BRITISH RAILWAYS
18

Far left, top: No 13 *Carisbrooke* (ex-LB&SC Class A1X No 77 *Wonersh*) at Ventnor West in 1948.

Far left, bottom: Train from Ryde entering Ventnor in 1948. 0-4-4T No 18 *Ningwood* ex-L&SW Class 02.

Above: Ryde Pier Head to Shanklin electric train composed of ex-London Transport 4-VEC units leaving Ryde in 1977.

Centre left: British Railways (Sealink) passenger ferry MV *Brading* (986, '48) leaving Portsmouth for Ryde in 1977.

Bottom left: I of W Lymington-Yarmouth vehicle and passenger ferry MV *Cenwulf* (761, '73).

London & South Western: South Western Division

The London & South Western Railway was the largest and most affluent of the three companies comprising the Southern Railway. Its route mileage of 862 began at Waterloo, Britain's largest passenger station and, passing through Basingstoke, Salisbury and Exeter, ended at Plymouth (Friary) in the South and Padstow on the North Cornwall coast. It served Portsmouth through an important branch which left the main line at Woking and Southampton, Bournemouth and Weymouth by an even more important branch which turned south from the main line at Worting Junction, some two miles west of Basingstoke. The last steeply graded six miles of this line between Dorchester and Weymouth were owned by the Great Western but over which the L&SW had running powers.

Generally speaking the old L&SW lines east of Salisbury have no very severe gradients but on the Bournemouth line there is a gradient of 1 in 250 almost continuously for 18 miles in the up direction after leaving Eastleigh. Also, on the Portsmouth line the ruling gradient is 1 in 80 for a short distance. None of these can compare with the climbing which has to be done west of Salisbury, but even so the steepest and most difficult routes on the L&SW were west of Exeter and were abandoned 15 years ago. Notable among those old lines was the 14½ mile section between Barnstaple Town and Ilfracombe which in the down direction had four miles almost continuously at 1 in 40 — 1 in 45 while up trains were faced with two miles at 1 in 36 on leaving Ilfracombe. Only the West Highland line has comparable hills to climb.

All the remaining South Western lines west of Salisbury are now included in British Railways' Western Region but in some sort of exchange, the Dorchester-Weymouth line is now Southern and the Channel Islands boat trains leave from Waterloo, being diesel hauled.

The L&SW was served by some of Britain's most distinguished railwaymen and the names of Sam Fay, Herbert Walker and the Szlumpers, father and son are well-remembered by those whose interest is in railways. On the locomotive side, Beattie, Adams, Drummond and Urie may be even better known by railway enthusiasts. Many were the innovations made by these men, the water tube boilers of Drummond and the fine fleet of mixed traffic locomotives produced by Urie are common knowledge. What is less well-known was the installation under Sam Fay's Superintendency of the first main line automatic signals in Britain to be controlled by track circuit.

When the Grouping of the railways took place in 1923, the Southern was by far the weakest, poorest and most rundown of the 'Big Four'. It was remarkable that, under the inspired leadership of Herbert Walker of the London & South Western, a team of hard-working and enthusiastic railway-men succeeded in making their railway one of the most efficient and well-run of all European railways.

In 1892 the L&SW purchased Southampton Docks, a most wise and far-sighted move. Improvements and extensions to the docks began almost immediately and many transatlantic and other passenger liner services were transferred from Liverpool. The enlarge-ment of the port was continued in Southern Railway days culminating in the Western Docks extensions made on reclaimed land and the construction of the largest graving dock in the world, the King George V Dock, opened in 1933. Furthermore, at the time of the 1923 Grouping the L&SW had its own fleet of some 14 ships operating passenger and cargo services between Southampton, le Havre, Cherbourg, St Malo and the Channel Islands. In 1978 there are few passenger liners visiting the port and the most important traffic is in the huge container ships. Equally large oil tankers berth alongside the refinery at Fawley.

Electrification of the L&SW suburban services began in 1915 the decision for this having been made for much the same reasons that lay behind earlier LB&SC schemes — the increasing competition from the bus and electric tram services of the London County Council. Unlike the LB&SC, however, the L&SW already had District Line trains running over some sections of its track. As these trains collected 660V direct current from a 'third rail' it was rational for the L&SW to follow the same practice. Thus began the extensive third rail electrification which now serves most of the Southern Region of British Railways. The most important electrification schemes to be made in former L&SW territory are those between Waterloo and Portsmouth completed by the Southern in 1937 and Waterloo to Bournemouth completed by British Railways in 1967. Traffic between Bournemouth and Weymouth does not justify the expense of electrification and instead this is operated by push-and-pull trains formed from sections of the electric expresses terminating at Bournemouth Central. The motive power is provided by Class 33 diesel electric Bo-Bo locomotives which 'pull' from Bournemouth to Weymouth and 'push' in the up direction. The load is normally four or eight corridor coaches.

My own roamings on the South Western have been made mostly since World War II. Before then I did quite a lot of photography of locomotives and trains in the West Country but regretfully, made no effort to obtain engine passes. However, I certainly made good the deficiency in later years and during the 1950s I rode a great variety of locomotives over nearly the whole territory of the South West. My most outstanding memory concerns a rebuilt 'Merchant Navy', No 35028 *Clan Line* working the 425 ton 10-car up 'Bournemouth Belle' from Bournemouth West. The regulator was so stiff that it took two men to open it at all and then it could be opened only to something between one quarter and one third of full. My locomotive inspector was in favour of asking for another engine at Southampton. The driver was in favour of carrying on. In the end the driver prevailed and this remarkable locomotive brought its train into Waterloo a bare 2½ minutes late and this was due to our having adverse signals all the way in from Vauxhall. With the boiler pressure maintained at 240-250psi the steam chest pressure was never above 110psi and the cut-off was between 20% and 30%. This most remarkable tribute to a very well-designed locomotive made one wonder if some of the high boiler pressures used in modern designs were really necessary.

There is one important preservation line in the South Western Division. This is the Mid-Hants Railway which operates between Alresford and Ropley about three miles of the former Alton-Winchester Junction line, the so-called 'Watercress Line'. The Mid-Hants was opened in 1977 and the available locomotives are a Class N 2-6-0 No 31874, now named *Aznar Line* and a Hunslet 0-6-0ST built in 1953 and formerly working on the Longmoor Military Railway which was closed in 1969. This locomotive still carries its LMR number 196 but its name, *Errol Lonsdale* has not been perpetuated. The Mid-Hants Railway owns several other locomotives, including two 'West Country' class at present under repair.

In 1875 the London & South Western and the Midland Railway became equal lessors of the Somerset & Dorset Joint Railway which ran between Bath and Bournemouth (West) with a branch from Evercreech Junction to Burnham-on-Sea. This fascinating railway abounded in severe curves, and very steep gradients, for example, five miles at 1 in 50, almost unbroken, between Evercreech and Masbury. More than 60 of its 105 route miles were single track. The Midland was responsible for locomotives, carriages and wagons and the L&SW looked after all civil engineering. On nationalisation, in 1948, the S&DJ became part of the Southern Region and, despite its importance as a link in the through services between Bournemouth and Manchester, Liverpool, Newcastle and other northern cities, the line was closed in 1966.

Above: A bowler-hatted locomotive inspector at Waterloo casts a critical eye on Class H15 No 334 which is about to work a down express for Salisbury and Exeter in 1936.

Right: Down 'Atlantic Coast Express' near Vauxhall in 1949. No 35005 *Canadian Pacific* was fitted with a mechanical stoker.

Below right: No 21C15 *Rotterdam Lloyd* in immaculate condition, was photographed in 1948 at the head of the down 'Devon Belle Pullman' near Vauxhall.

Above left: Rebuilt Drummond 4-cylinder 'Paddlebox' No 458 on a down slow train for Salisbury approaching Walton in 1938.

Left: 'King Arthur' class No 455 *Sir Launcelot* heading a down West of England express past Walton in 1936.

Below: Class S15 No 30503 passing Basingstoke locomotive sheds with a down main line freight in 1961.

34049
34049
30503
439
30433
30433

Far left, top: 'Battle of Britain' 4-6-2 No 34049 *Anti-Aircraft Command* leaving Basingstoke with an express for Plymouth in 1952 while Class S15 No 30503 on a freight for Salisbury takes water at the adjoining platform.

Far left, bottom: Heading a down train of bogie hopper wagons for Meldon Quarry, Class L12 No 30433 was passing Basingstoke in 1951.

Top left: Waterloo to Exeter express entering Basingstoke. Class 33/1 Bo-Bo diesel-electric No 33.107.

Centre left: Reading to Salisbury train leaving Basingstoke. Diesel-electric 3-car unit No 1131.

Below: Down main line freight leaving Basingstoke hauled by Bo-Bo diesel-electric No D6585 (later Class 33/0 No 33.065).

Top left: Waterloo station in 1955 with No 30859 *Lord Hood* leaving with an express for Bournemouth.

Centre left: Class H16 No 30519 with empty stock from Waterloo arriving at Clapham Junction in 1951.

Below: Passing West Weybridge in 1948 with the down 'Bournemouth Belle' was No 21C17 *Belgian Marine*

Top right: Heading the up 'Bournemouth Belle' near Eastleigh in 1951 was Class 7 4-6-2 No 70009 *Alfred the Great*

Centre right: Ex-LMS Class 3 Co-Co diesel-electric No 10000 on down Bournemouth express near Swaythling in 1953.

Bottom right: BR Class 4 4-6-0 No 75007 takes water at Basingstoke before proceeding to Bournemouth with a special train from the north. A 1959 picture.

70009.
THE
BOURNEMOUTH
BELLE

10000

75007

Above: Birmingham-Bournemouth Inter-City express near Shawford. Class 33/1 Bo-Bo diesel-electric No 33.129.

Centre right: 'Schools' class No 30911 *Dover* working a down Bournemouth train through West Weybridge in 1954.

Bottom right: Standard Class 5 No 73085 on a Waterloo-Bournemouth express passing West Weybridge in 1959.

Far right, top: Headed by No 929 *Malvern* with multiple jet exhaust this down Bournemouth express was passing Byfleet when photographed in 1947.

Far right, centre: Class 33/1 Bo-Bo diesel-electric No 33.114 passing Winchester with a train of Ford commercial vehicles from the Eastleigh factory.

Far right, bottom: Eastleigh steam shed with a 'foreigner' on view.

92

Winchester
HO

76019

92

Left: The erecting shop at Eastleigh Works on a Sunday when steam still worked on the Southern.

Bottom left: Waterloo-Bournemouth and Weymouth express passing Eastleigh. The two leading 4-TC trailer units will be detached at Bournemouth and worked to Weymouth by a Class 33/1 diesel-electric locomotive.

Top right: 'King Arthur' No 30784 *Sir Nerovens* fitted with a spark arresting chimney was heading a down Bournemouth express in 1953 near Swaythling.

Centre right: Block train of Amalgamated Rockstone empty hopper wagons in charge of Class 47 Co-Co diesel-electric No 47.147 near Southampton Airport.

Below: BR Standard Class 3MT 2-6-2T No 82012 working a freight for Fawley through Southampton Central in 1953.

Above: No 30486, one of Urie's Class H15 was heading a fast train for Bournemouth when photographed leaving Southampton Central in 1953.

Right: When the 'King Arthurs' were scrapped, nameplates from some of them were given to BR Standard Class 5 4-6-0s. No 73114 carried the name *Etarre* from No 30751 in 1960.

Below right: Portsmouth to Salisbury train leaving Southampton in 1953. Standard Class 4 2-6-2 No 76013.

Above: A proud and historic day for the Southern Railway. The new SS *Queen Mary* (81237 '36) about to enter the King George V graving dock before her official trials on 20 March 1936. Also seen is the new Southern train ferry *Hampton Ferry* and, right, the White Star liner *Majestic.*

Left: The Western Docks extension at Southampton. The gate gives access to Herbert Walker Avenue named after the Southern Railway Chairman.

Below left: Southampton Ocean Dock with, left, Cunard SS *Queen Elizabeth 2* (65863 '68) and, right, Russian SS *Leonid Sobinov* (21370 '54) ex-Cunard *Carmania.*

Above right: Class 74 Bo-Bo electro-diesel No 74.004 on boat train for SS *Leonid Sobinov* passing Chapel Crossing, Southampton before entering the docks.

Right: Class 33/0 Bo-Bo diesel-electric No 33.013 on empty *Leonid Sobinov* boat train stock leaving the quayside at Southampton.

Below: Ruston diesel-electric 0-6-0 Class 07 No 07.001 heading empty *Australis* boat train stock at Queen Elizabeth II Terminal, Southampton.

Above left: Freightliner's Maritime Container Terminal at Southampton. Class 47/3 Co-Co diesel-electric No 47.332 arriving with a train of 'boxes' from Barking. Centre: some of the flat cars awaiting loading. Right: containers loaded on road vehicles awaiting road haulage to the dockside a few hundred yards away.

Left: Container express from Southampton Maritime Terminal to Coatbridge passing Micheldever. Class 47/0 Co-Co diesel-electric No 47.051.

Below: It was nearly the 'end of the line' for No 34090 formerly *Sir Eustace Missenden* when it was photographed leaving Bournemouth with an up train in 1967. Number and nameplates had been removed to prevent their being stolen.

Left: Class 47/0 Co-Co diesel-electric No 47.033 on train of empty 4-wheeled tank wagons leaving Micheldever for Aldermaston.

Below left: Standard Class 9 2-10-0 No 92248 with a train of oil tanks from Fawley passing Eastleigh in 1961.

Top right: Class 47/3 Co-Co diesel-electric No 47.350 on up train of bogie oil tank wagons from Fawley passing Shawford. In the right background are hollow blocks used in the construction of floating harbours.

Centre right: North British 0-4-0 diesel-mechanical yard locomotive hauling a train of empty 4-wheeled tank wagons into the Esso Refinery at Fawley.

Below: Class 33/0 Bo-Bo diesel-electric No 33.006 arriving at Fawley with empty 4-wheeled tank wagons.

Right: The Channel Islands boat train from Waterloo, on reaching Weymouth passes down Commercial Road to reach the docks. It is preceded first by a police car . . .

Below: . . . followed by two pilotmen walking in front of the Bo-Bo diesel-electric locomotive, in this case Class 33/1 No 33.109 fitted with a bell.

Top left: Weymouth Harbour with Sealink steamships *Sarnia* (4174, '61) *Maid of Kent* (3920, '59) and *Caledonian Princess* (3630, '61). The last two of these are car ferries.

Centre left: Leaving Weymouth in 1977, the car ferry SS *Maid of Kent* (3920, '59) which was built for the Dover cross-channel services. As she loads only through the stern she was sent to Weymouth for the Channel Islands and the Cherbourg services.

Below: Two 4-car trailer units propelled by Class 33/1 Bo-Bo diesel-electric No 33.119 leaving Wool en route from Weymouth to Bournemouth (and Waterloo).

41304
41304

30729
371

82014

Far left, top: Ex-LMS 2-6-2T No 41304 at the now closed Southampton Terminus station in 1952 with a train for Cheltenham.

Far left, centre: Train from Portsmouth to Salisbury leaving Fareham in 1957. Rebuilt and superheated Class T9 4-4-0 No 30729.

Far left, bottom: Southampton to Portsmouth train approaching Fareham in 1957 headed by BR Class 3MT 2-6-2T No 82014.

Top left: Hythe pier in Hampshire (opposite Southampton) is 700 yards long and is served by a 2ft-gauge electric railway. The locomotive propels the train on the outward journey (as seen here) a driving compartment being provided in the leading coach. The 4-wheeled locomotive is chain driven by four 5½hp traction motors which collect current from a third rail at 200V dc. Speed is 12mph.

Centre left: Ex-LMS 2-6-2T No 41295 with taper chimney on a van train at Clapham Junction in 1952.

Below: Far away from its usual London suburban duties Class M7 No 30242 was heading an Eastleigh to Salisbury via Redbridge train near Swaythling in 1950.

82035

M
31912

Top left: BR Class 3MT 2-6-2T was pilot to Class No 31853 working a heavy train of Meldon Quarry stone between Exeter St David's and Exeter Central in 1964.

Centre left: Two 0-6-2T Nos 32124 and 2697 Class E1R about to bank an express for Waterloo up the 1 in 37 from Exeter St David's to Exeter Central in 1949.

Bottom left: Banking an up express between Exeter St David's and Exeter Central in 1962 was Class W 2-6-4T No 31912.

Top right: No 21C2 *Union Castle* on a down express climbing the 1 in 80 Honiton Incline in 1948.

Centre right: On a Wenford freight passing Boscarne Junction in 1950 was ex-L&SW Class 0298 2-4-0T No 30585 with a Drummond boiler.

Below: One of my favourite photographs shows ex-PD&SWJR 0-6-2T, Southern No 758 *Lord St Levan*, on a Bere Alston to Callington freight at the summit of this steeply graded line near Chilsworthy in 1949.

Above: Mid-Hants Railway: preparing for the day's work at Alresford. Class N No 31874 *Aznar Line* and 0-6-0ST No 196.

Right: Mid-Hants Railway: 0-6-0ST No 196 ex-Longmoor Military Railway heading a train from Alresford to Ropley.

Below right: Mid-Hants Railway: 0-6-0ST No 196 with a train for Alresford at Ropley.

Above: S&DJ 4-4-0 No 40634 (old No 45) and BR Class 5 No 73051 on a Manchester to Bournemouth train passing Chilcompton in 1954.

Left: S&DJ No 40634 piloting No 34110 *66 Squadron* on a Bournemouth to Manchester train passing Masbury in 1953.

Below left: S&DJ: Running fast down the 1 in 50 gradient approaching Chilcompton in 1954 was a begrimed 2-8-0 No 53805 with a Bournemouth to Sheffield train.

Foreigners

Below: Southern in Scotland. Caledonian 0-6-0 No 381 (LMS 17101) built by Neilson in 1868 for the LC&DR but was sold to the Solway Junction Railway in 1869 and came into Caledonian stock in 1870.

Bottom: Scotland on the Southern. Preserved Caledonian 7ft 4-2-2 No 123 (Neilson 1886) was at Stewart's Lane shed in June 1953 for a Royal Train exhibition at Battersea wharf.

To most railway enthusiasts the workings of locomotives outside their normal spheres of operation are events of some importance. For example, the appearance of a Caledonian locomotive at Stewart's Lane or of a 'Deltic' at Dover are matters which certainly require photographic attention.

This chapter deals with some of the visitors we have seen on the Southern Region and with the appearances of Southern locomotives on other regions. Railwaymen often refer to these visitors as 'foreigners' but the visits of some locomotives to regions other than their own are so regular and frequent that they are no longer exceptional or worthy of special note. The regular working in Southern territory of Class 47 diesel-electrics from other regions is a case in point.

The period when foreign workings were most interesting was during the locomotive exchanges of 1948 when efforts were being made to determine the best designs for future construction. There were, however, some interchanges during the period which were not so widely known as were those of the main line locomotives. On the Southern there was the trial of the LMS 2-6-4T locomotives which resulted in the wide adoption of these engines in the region. Conversely, the trials of the Southern 'West Country' class on the former Great Eastern lines of the Eastern Region resulted in their firm (and not always polite) rejection.

Above: Foreigners in more senses than one! Some of the WD 'Austerity' 2-8-0s assembled at Richborough Port, Kent, on being returned from the Continent in 1946.

Left: 'Merchant Navy' class No 35019 *French Line CGT* with LMS tender heading an up Plymouth express passing Hayes on the Western Region during the Locomotive Exchange of 1948.

Below left: Great Western dynamometer car behind 'Merchant Navy' class No 35018 *British India Line* on the down 'Atlantic Coast Express' at Waterloo during the Locomotive Exchanges of 1948.

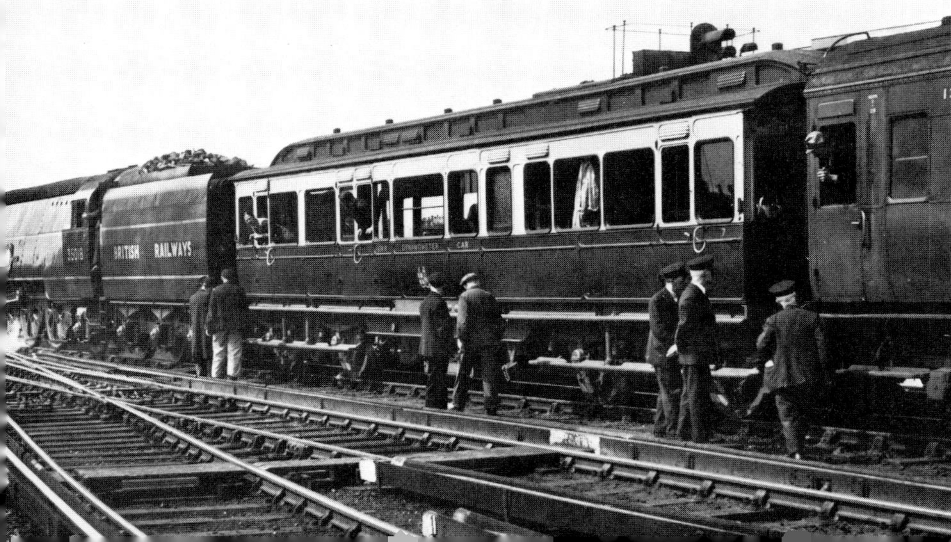

42199
BRITISH RAILWAYS

Above left: Ex-LMS 4-6-2 No 46236 *City of Bradford* with ROD 8-wheeled tender on the up 'Atlantic Coast Express' near Vauxhall during the 1948 Locomotive Exchanges.

Centre left: Ex-LMS 2-6-4T No 42199 on trial on the Southern in 1948 with an up special train leaving Ashford.

Bottom left: Class B1 ex-LNE 4-6-0 No 61015 *Duiker* on down Ramsgate Pullman Car express on the Reculver sea-wall in 1953. A number of these engines (and some Class V2 2-6-2s) were loaned to the Southern when cracks were found in the crank axles of some Southern Region Pacifics.

Above: Preserved GW 4-4-0 No 3440 *City of Truro* working a special train leaving Eastleigh for Swindon Town in 1957.

Centre right: A regular foreign working was that of the Bulleid Pacifics with the 'Pines Express' between Bournemouth and Oxford. Leaving Oxford with the southbound train (Manchester-Bournemouth) in 1963 was rebuilt 'Battle of Britain' No 34053 *Sir Keith Park*.

Bottom right: Southern Region diesels on the old GN main line. Type 2 Bo-Bo Nos D6573 and D6578 (later Class 33/1) heading a train of Cemflow cement empties from Uddingston to Cliffe north of Potters Bar in 1962.

Above: 'Deltic' Class 55 Co-Co diesel-electric No 55.007 *Pinza* headed a special train from Victoria round Kent and part of Sussex on 26 March 1978. This was the first recorded instance of a 'Deltic' working on the Southern. The train was photographed leaving Dover Marine.

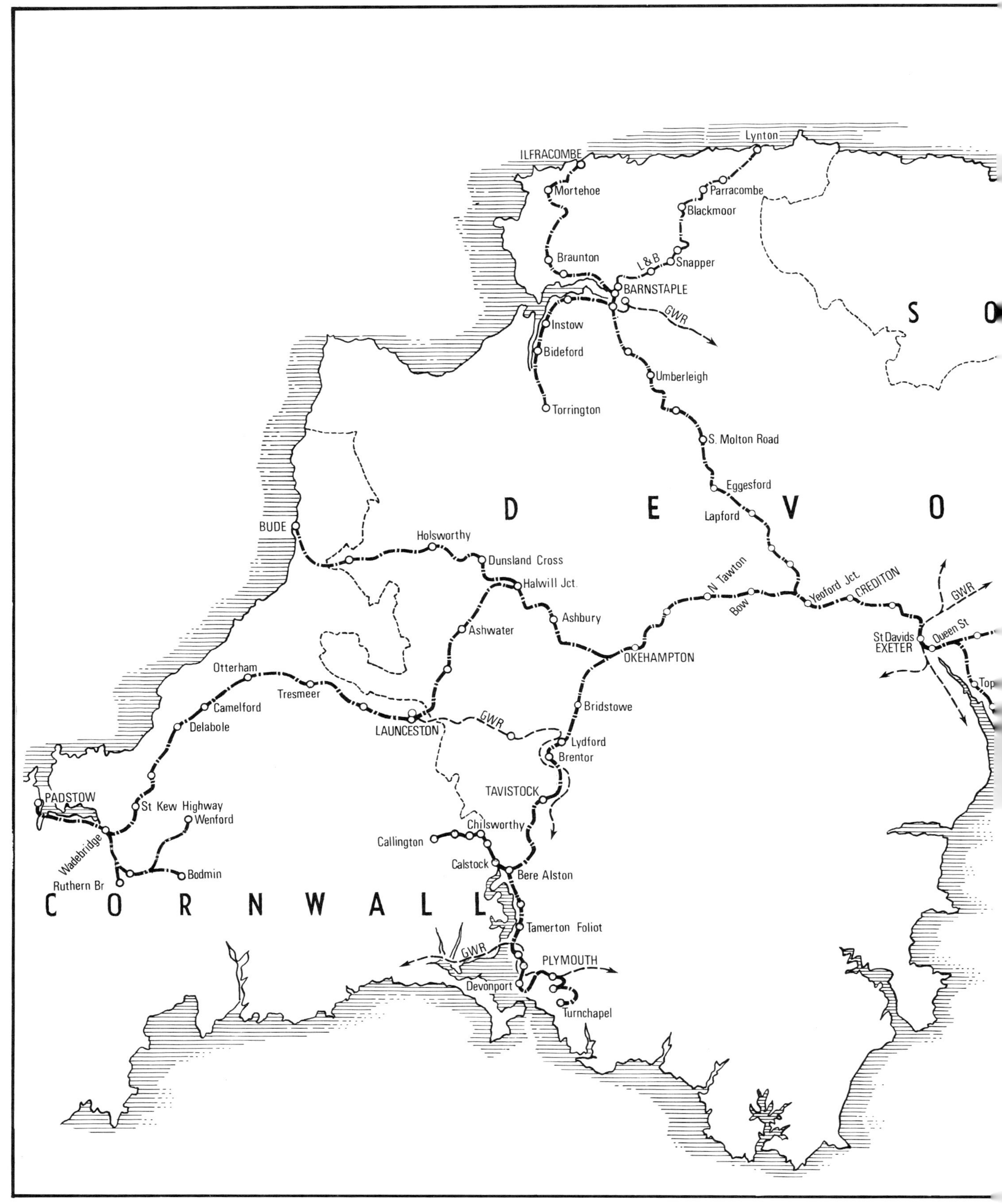

ILFRACOMBE
Lynton
Mortehoe
Parracombe
Blackmoor
Braunton
L&B
Snapper
BARNSTAPLE
GWR
Instow
Bideford
Umberleigh
Torrington
S. Molton Road
Eggesford
Lapford
D E V O
BUDE
Holsworthy
Dunsland Cross
Halwill Jct.
N Tawton
Bow
Yeoford Jct.
CREDITON
GWR
Ashbury
Ashwater
OKEHAMPTON
St Davids
EXETER
Queen St
Otterham
Tresmeer
Camelford
Delabole
LAUNCESTON
GWR
Bridstowe
Lydford
Brentor
TAVISTOCK
PADSTOW
St Kew Highway
Wenford
Wadebridge
Chilsworthy
Callington
Calstock
Bere Alston
Bodmin
Ruthern Br
C O R N W A L L
Tamerton Foliot
GWR
PLYMOUTH
Devonport
Turnchapel